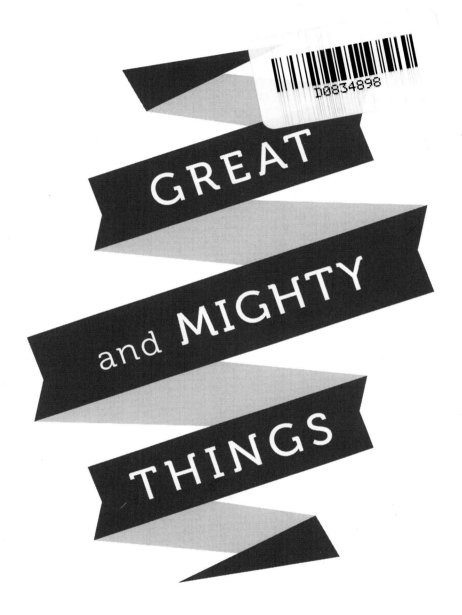

GREAT
and MIGHTY
THINGS

PASTOR **CHUCK BOOHER**

Table of Contents

Introduction

Call to Me and I will answer you, and I will tell you great and mighty things, which you do not know. **Jeremiah 33:3 (NASB)**

I prayed fervently before writing this book, wanting to be sure that it would enhance the Kingdom of God and not be a selfish endeavor. God assured me that it was a story that needed to be told because it could change lives and provide much-needed wisdom and encouragement to church leaders. Ultimately, this story gives glory to God. He did great and mighty things in our church as we called out to Him and followed Him on this journey. As you read this story, I hope you see that the only reason Crossroads exists today is because our God chose to work in us and through us that He might be glorified.

My goal in writing this book is to lead you to a life of great and mighty things. God's Word is filled with so many wonderful promises and yet many Christians miss out on those promises and live ordinary mundane lives. My journey with God has never been boring. Life with Him, even through the challenges, is thrilling. In reading this book, I hope your eyes are opened to the exciting, fulfilling, and extraordinary life God describes in His Word. Great and mighty things await you.

Leadership Lessons

Throughout this book, you will find sections entitled **"Leadership Lessons."** These are lessons that God taught me during my journey as the leader of Crossroads Christian Church. I have had the privilege of being around many great leaders who stretch me and challenge me to grow in my leadership ability. One thing I've observed in all of them is their appetite for knowledge and wisdom.

I had just finished having dinner with the CEO of one of the top financial institutions in the nation, and we were outside the restaurant waiting with the valet for our car. Before I knew it, my friend had struck up a conversation with this young college-aged man and was asking him all kinds of questions about his job as a valet, why he enjoyed working there, his aspirations, and his career path. This successful CEO learned a lot from that young man that evening, and I learned even more from my friend about leadership.

A great leader will learn in every situation and from every encounter. Christ followers will do the same. The promise of Jeremiah 33:3 says that God will "tell" us great and mighty things. He will teach us.

Behold, God is exalted in His power; Who is a teacher like Him? - **Job 36:22 (NASB)**

God is our teacher and we need to be clothed in humility and ready to learn from Him through His Word and through the people He puts in our path.

Although the Lord has given you bread of privation and water of oppression, He, your Teacher will no longer hide Himself, but your eyes will behold your Teacher. Your ears will hear a word behind you, "This is the way, walk in it," whenever you turn to the right or to the left.
                              - Isaiah 30:20-21 (NASB)

Leadership Lesson:

Leaders are learners!

5

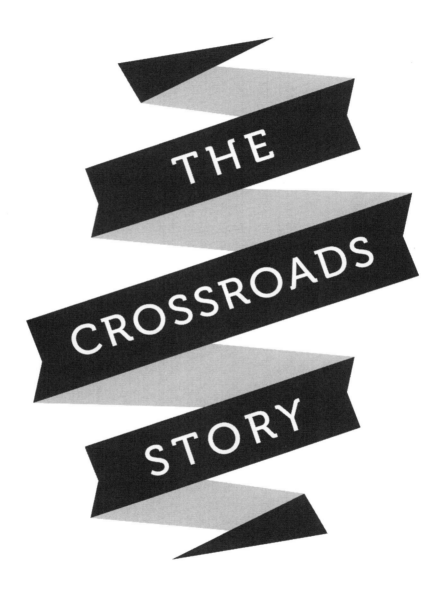

PART ONE

THE CROSSROADS STORY

Chapter One

The Crucible

The crucible is for silver, and the furnace is for gold, and the LORD tests hearts. **Proverbs 17:3 (ESV)**

As I lay in bed, my body shook uncontrollably from the overwhelming stress of what the future had in store. I was living in a nightmare; a nightmare that I had chosen to step into. I used to be the Senior Pastor of a thriving mega-church and now I was the Senior Pastor of a church on the brink of foreclosure. I left a place that promised me complete financial security to come to this place that could not promise me tomorrow's paycheck. The church I left, loved me deeply. Many people on this church's staff loathed me. I stood at the base of this daunting mountain of mess and wondered if it was even possible to climb it.

*But He said, "The things that are impossible with people are possible with God." - **Luke 18:27***

I knew beyond a shadow of a doubt, that I was exactly where God wanted me.

The Beginning

It all began with a phone call from Brad Dupray, the Chairman of the elders at Crossroads Christian Church, asking me if I would be interested in becoming their Senior Pastor when Senior Pastor Barry McMurtrie retired. My wife, Pam, and I loved Crossroads and considered it our church home. Many of our significant life-changing moments took place at that church: it was where we first met Christ, were called into the ministry, and were married. However, I didn't feel called to leave my current church at this time. But, Brad insisted and we agreed to pray about it. We requested the church's statistics and financial statements from him in order to get a better picture of the church. Brad hesitated and proceeded to inform me that he was not sure if he'd be able to provide me with that information because the church was having issues with its current leadership. The elder board of Crossroads did not feel as though they were being given an accurate financial picture by the church staff. He promised to be more assertive in obtaining this information and would get back to me.

Later that week, God provided Brad with a divine appointment when he walked into the Crossroads church offices. Two accountants who he knew personally were in the office at the time that he arrived. They informed him that they were performing an audit on the church that was not going well. The church was in serious financial trouble and as the Chairman of the Elders, they felt it was important that he knew the financial status of the church.

As Brad dug deeper into the financial documents, he discovered many unpaid bills, including a mortgage in danger of foreclosure. In an effort to stop the bleeding of this financial mess, he arranged for the bank to give Crossroads a third mortgage loan for one million dollars. The money could only be used to make mortgage payments on the first loan to the bank. This one million dollars quickly went down to nearly half the amount after getting caught up on the past unpaid mortgage payments. No one - not the board, the staff, or the congregation knew the gravity of the situation.

Prior to the first conversation I had with Brad, Pastor Barry had arranged for me to come and fill in to preach for him while he was on vacation. When the day came for me to preach at Crossroads, I felt confident that Crossroads was not where God wanted me at this time in my life. My plan was to fill in for Pastor Barry that one week and then go back to my amazing church where they were, at that moment, working on a comfortable retirement package for me.

God had a different plan.

I preached and God moved. The people were hungry for more of Him and were eating all that I had to offer them from His Word. At the end of my sermon, I gave an invitation for people to accept Christ as Lord and Savior. People flooded forward to accept this invitation. I looked over at my wife who was in tears because of the moving of the Holy Spirit in that place. I walked over to her and she whispered to me, "God wants you here." Terror gripped me.

It made absolutely no sense for me to leave Christ's Church of the Valley, CCV, where I had been for the past 19 years. The people there were our family, we had an amazing elder board, and a fun staff. The church was growing and was financially solid which allowed me to dream big dreams.

Why would anyone in his or her right mind leave such a wonderful place to go to a church that was on the brink of disaster?

I continued to delve into the disastrous financial details of Crossroads, trying to convince God that He did not want me to go. I'll never forget the night I came home and told Pam that there was no way we could go to Crossroads. Things were so bad there that it was inevitable that they would not be able to pay us, and we would lose our house. She looked at me with a steady gaze and resolutely replied, "Then, we are going. We have never been in ministry for money. We are not for sale. We are going to Crossroads."

Our decision was made.

I met with the elder board one last time to finalize all the details and clarify expectations. During this meeting we continued to ascertain the depth of the hole in which the church found itself. The elders found out that they were technically Trustees of the church, which meant that their personal assets could be at stake if the church did not make it. Organizations usually have insurance for situations like these, but our insurance had been cancelled because it went unpaid.

It was important for me in the midst of the mess to make sure that they knew what they were getting in a pastor when I came on board. I let the board know if I came, I would bring a clear and challenging mission statement to the church, I would have complete control and oversight of the staff, we would be a church committed to outreach beyond our walls, and my preaching was not up for vote.

My life goal is to be passionately committed to Christ, His cause, and His community. I strive to love Christ and be like Him; to seek and save the lost and help those in need; and to be a vital part of the Church at large and in fellowship with believers for mutual accountability and edification. This personal mission statement would become the mission statement of Crossroads and would be the expectation of each member of the church.

Having complete control and oversight of the staff was vital to my effectiveness. I knew layoffs were inevitable and I needed complete authority to make employee decisions and to build my team. We had an uphill battle ahead of us and I needed soldiers who would stay focused and keep climbing with me. The board would not be able to make these types of decisions for me because without working with the staff daily, they would not have an accurate assessment of them.

Another condition of my acceptance of the position was the elders' agreement to be a church committed to outreach beyond our walls. We would be a church with a substantial missions program and would specifically support the work that Pam and I had started in Kenya through CCV. God had asked us to make a difference in Kenya during our ministry at CCV and I wanted to continue to be faithful in that assignment.

Finally, I needed the elders to agree that my preaching would not be up for vote. God and I determine my sermons because I cannot effectively preach if I seek to please people. I explained to them that there would be times when I preach what people need to hear as opposed to what they want to hear. There would also be occasions when I preach something that they might disagree with, but I needed the authority to preach what God reveals to me through my study of His Word. They could be sure that I would never preach something contrary to our statement of faith, but the bottom line was that I preach to please God and not people.

For am I now seeking the favor of men, or of God? Or am I striving to please men? If I were still trying to please men, I would not be a bond-servant of Christ. - **Galatians 1:10**

Pam and I left the meeting while the elders stayed and discussed my conditions. We drove to Crossroads and sat in the parking lot praying for God's will to be done and for Him to prepare us for the journey ahead if the elders offered me the position. Before we said "amen," my cell phone rang. The elders unanimously decided that I was the new Senior Pastor of Crossroads Christian Church. Getting a new job is usually exciting, but this situation was different. I felt like I just stepped into a roller coaster blindfolded. God was about to take me on a wild adventure.

Chapter Two

Trials and Transparency

Blessed is a man who perseveres under trial; for once he has been approved, he will receive the crown of life which the Lord has promised to those who love Him. **James 1:12 (NASB)**

My First Day

You know those television shows where they play jokes on people just to watch them lose their cool and laugh at their reaction to a really uncomfortable and bizarre situation? By the end of my first day in the office at Crossroads, I was sure that the hidden cameras were going to pop out at any minute and tell me that the whole day was a joke.

There was no welcome committee, no flowers, no friendly faces to greet me when I walked into the office for my first day of work. Instead, a cold office in disarray greeted me. Every other office door was closed while the people to whom they belonged isolated themselves inside. The entire place felt cold and devoid of joy and love. I missed the warmth of CCV.

While trying to make sense of my disheveled office, Blake Ryan came in to deliver the first of many pieces of bad news that day. Blake is a genius in finance who loves the Lord and had agreed to come onto the Crossroads staff to help us make sense of the financial mess and come up with a plan to get out of the situation. At one point, the stress would take such a huge physical toll on his body that he would end up in the hospital. This particular morning, Blake informed me that the projector in our main worship center was a rental and the rent had not been paid. The company would be repossessing it before our weekend services which was problematic because the Crossroads Worship Center is a huge building which seats over 3,000 people. It was designed to have projection in order for people to connect with the speaker. I decided to take the "glass half full" approach: the absence of a projector would prove to the congregation that the church was truly in a dire financial situation.

While I was still mulling over having a church service with no projector, I heard shouting coming from the hallway outside of my office. I walked out to see two people on our staff angrily yelling at each other. I was stunned that people on a church staff would talk to each other in such a disrespectful manner. When they saw me watching them, they stopped, embarrassed at their blatant unprofessional behavior. I walked back into my office to strategize how to repair this sinking ship. Before I could even begin to sort out my thoughts, Blake came in with another dose of bad news. Our checking account was $27,000.00 in the red. How was that possible? He informed me that the previous leadership was taking money that was promised to go to orphans in India and paying salaries instead. Blake left to go dig up more bad news. All too soon, he was back to report his findings. Our electric company had just notified him that they were going to shut off our electricity unless we came up with $85,000 by Friday. Now, I was confident that I could do a weekend service with no projector, but I knew that there was no way I could do a weekend service without electricity. Our worship center has no windows and I could not safely have the people in the building without electricity. I was overwhelmed and needed to take a walk and talk to God.

I walked outside and asked the Lord to give me some relief. I noticed a woman coming my way and thought, *Thank you Lord. She will be my answer. I am sure that she is an angel that you've sent to me at this time to give us a million dollars. Or, perhaps she is a lost soul coming on this church campus to find Jesus and will be my first convert.* Upon greeting her, I discovered that she was neither an angel nor a searching soul. She was an inspector from the Health Department informing me that our café, which was connected to our children's building, was infested with rodents and was being shut down immediately.

As if on cue, seconds after the health inspector walked away, Cesar our Director of Facilities, came running up to me frantically telling me to hide. I asked, "Why?" "The city water department is here to shut off the water and wants to speak to the person in charge. I am trying to tell them that you are new and convince them to give you a break. If you hide, it might buy us some more time," Cesar replied. I did what any respectable leader would do -- I hid.

Where were the hidden cameras? They had let this joke go too far. It was time for them to jump out and tell me that I was on some sort of television show, now.

Telling the Church

How do you tell a wonderful unsuspecting congregation that the finances of their church are a mess and that many of the things that they had been told about the finances were untrue? One week they would be saying good-bye to a Pastor they loved and the next week would be told by the new guy that the church needed to beg God for His intervention because the church was weeks away from closing its doors. Wouldn't they all leave the church out of frustration and anger?

I was not equipped to handle this situation, but I personally knew the One who is equipped to handle every situation. He reminded me that Crossroads was His Church. It was a church with a rich 115-year history, which He had used in great and mighty ways to draw people to Him. In spite of the bleak horizon, I chose to believe that He was not done with this church.

With my new resolve, I began to draw up a strategy to inform the church. I would start by informing the most influential people in the church and ask them to be on my team to help me carry the message in a positive way to the rest of the church. I asked our Stewardship Director, Lisa Mitchison, who had a relationship with this group of people, to organize a meeting for the Thursday before my first weekend with the 100 most influential people at Crossroads. Lisa was an all-star. She organized a team of friendly people to invite everyone on her list and on the night of the event, she created a warm, inviting, and positive atmosphere.

I have always believed in transparency and felt it necessary to tell these people everything that we knew up to this moment. Blake worked around the clock to assimilate and organize in writing, the information to be presented at the meeting. It was absolutely necessary that the information be presented clearly and accurately.

There were three big issues that I felt needed to be revealed. The church believed that the Yamaha Piano that we used for worship every week had been donated to us. I was going to tell them that it was not donated and that we owed Yamaha $85,000 that we did not have. The church also believed that the beautifully lighted cell phone tower on our property was a source of revenue for us. I was going to tell them that we were actually paying someone else for the tower and because of the way the contract was written, we would never earn a penny from it. Finally, I would let them know that we had $185,000 of unpaid bills sitting in our accounting office with no way of paying them because we were $27,000 in the red in our checking account.

I prayed for God to reveal His words to me so that I would say only what He wanted me to say. I found Him to be faithful.

But if any of you lacks wisdom, let him ask of God, who gives to all generously and without reproach, and it will be given to him. - *James 1:5 (NASB)*

Every word which was spoken, every step taken and every action we did came from Him. At least the ones that worked. He did not leave us for one moment. He gave His wisdom generously.

The night of the meeting, people arrived filled with joy. They believed that they were there to meet their new Senior Pastor. Many greeted me warmly, welcoming me home. With each handshake and hug, I felt my stomach turn. I knew that in just moments I was going to turn their joy into sadness and possibly anger.

I walked up to the front of the crowded room and began the meeting. After welcoming them and praying for our time together, I let them know that I needed to share some very difficult information with them. I asked for the handout that Blake had created to be given to them and proceeded to go point by point through the information. I could hear gasps as people took in the shocking information. I saw their eyes fill with tears of hurt and my heart broke for them.

Before I opened it up for questions, I addressed the one question that I knew everyone wanted the answer to, "Who is responsible for this mess?" I had wrestled through this question with God prior to this meeting and knew exactly what he wanted me to say. "I know that you want to know who is responsible for these things. I am. I am the Senior Pastor of this church. I came here knowing this information. I am responsible." The silence was loud and I could feel the Holy Spirit moving in that room. I continued on, "Pam and I are here to be on this journey with you and to see this church move forward. I hope that you choose to join us." The room filled with applause; they were with us! I cautioned them against the bitterness that would try to make its way into their hearts and the temptation to play the blame game. I assured them that if I found out that something illegal was done, I would take appropriate action and be honest with them about it.

I concluded the night by telling them that they would play a vital part in getting the church out of this mess. First, I needed them to be intercessors for me. I implored them to pray for me and for the church daily, as this was a situation that could only be remedied by God, Himself. Next, I asked them to keep the information confidential until I shared it with the church at the congregational meeting. Finally, I asked them to attend the congregational meeting that I would be holding on the following Sunday night. They would be my team of information bearers who would protect against rumors and false information being spread. As I closed the night in prayer, I was overwhelmed by God's presence and the joy that filled that room.

Looking back now, I am amazed at the faithfulness of this group of people. They did everything I asked and are a huge reason why Crossroads is the vibrant church that it is today.

How Did All of This Happen?

How does a wonderful church get itself into such a deep ditch? I believe it happens very slowly. In this case, there were several individuals in leadership who made mistakes and the bigger the church got, the more devastating the results of those mistakes. I believe that they had the best of intentions, but did not fully understand the complexities of running a church this size. Sadly, they are the ones who got hurt the most. I prayed for them then and I continue to pray for them today.

My First Sunday

Something seemed off during my first Sunday morning worship services at Crossroads. My sermon went great and we had quite a few people respond to the invitation to come to Christ. We had 2,941 people in attendance and 500 children in our Children's Ministry. I was very happy with all of those numbers, but there was just something eerie about that morning. I couldn't quite pinpoint it, but I knew that I had never felt this way in any church I had ever been a part of or had visited. Little did I know that evil was lurking and God was making me aware of it.

Congregational Meeting

That night, 2,649 showed up for the Congregational meeting. There was a buzz of anticipation in the room. They all were curious as to what the new Senior Pastor was going to share with them. They had no idea about the bomb I had to drop on them.

I went on to teach the staff what the Bible says about conflict resolution. I pointed them to Matthew 5 and 18. There was so much animosity among the staff that even those who were spiritually mature were not handling conflict according to the principles described in these passages of Scripture. Instead of love and healthy conversations, I found clearly drawn battle lines, people demonized, and factions. In the Sermon on the Mount Jesus says,

Therefore if you are presenting your offering at the altar, and there remember that your brother has something against you, leave your offering there before the altar and go; first be reconciled to your brother, and then come and present your offering. - **Matthew 5:23-24**

If we know that someone has something against us, whether it is our fault or not, we are to go to them immediately. This is such a high priority that we are to do this "first;" before prayer and worship.

When we are the ones who have a grievance against someone, Jesus teaches us that we are to be the ones to go to that person to seek resolution.

If your brother sins, go and show him his fault in private; if he listens to you, you have won your brother. But if he does not listen to you, take one or two more with you, so that BY THE MOUTH OF TWO OR THREE WITNESSES EVERY FACT MAY BE CONFIRMED. If he refuses to listen to them, tell it to the church; and if he refuses to listen even to the church, let him be to you as a Gentile and a tax collector.

*- **Matthew 18:15-17***

I emphasized to the staff that we need to make it a practice to go *in private* to the one who hurt us. When we do this, we can say some of the most beautiful words ever heard, "I have not talked with anyone else about this."

At the end of that meeting, I drew a line in the sand. The staff had until April 15th to resolve any issues that they had with one another according to the principles I had just taught. I let them know that after that date, if I found out that people still had unresolved issues with one another, they would be fired.

The staff followed through and began to have these meetings with each other to work out the issues. These meetings turned into joyous occasions usually ending in happy tears and hugs. The atmosphere in the office began to change. I noticed that people were leaving their office doors open and were interacting and going to lunch together. The poison of bitterness had lost its power, and a spirit of joy took hold. By the time April 15th rolled around, our staff had risen to the occasion. They had honored and blessed God by loving one another. We were becoming united and were ready to overcome the problems ahead.

Cutting Spending

The first daunting step to cutting spending was the dreaded layoffs. I had been meeting with the staff as much as possible in my first few weeks in an effort to get to know them and their function on the church staff. Many of them were great people who were definitely not a part of the problem. Then, there were some who should have never been hired to be on a Christian church staff: non-Christians openly living in sin, Christians living with hidden sin, and people who had no idea how to do the job for which they'd been hired.

I remember meeting with one person to confront her about her living situation (she was living with her boyfriend). I told her that even if she was not sexually active with him, we could not have her on staff if she was living with him. She assured me that they were sexually active and saw no issue with it. I opened my Bible and shared with her how God clearly tells us that this is unacceptable behavior for a Christian because he has designed sex to be enjoyed in the context of marriage only. She casually leaned back in her chair and confidently informed me that this would not apply to her because she was not a Christian. I let her know that based on that confession, I would be letting her go. A look of pure shock and confusion came over her face. "Why?" she asked. "The very fact that you are asking 'Why?' is why," I responded.

Although this particular layoff was not a difficult one, most of the rest were going to be difficult. As I calculated the number that we would have to let go, my heart broke. I was going to have to lose some greatly gifted and effective people. There would be huge holes left in our ministries.

The week I began laying people off was one of the hardest of my life. I was unable to sleep at night and I begged God to show me a less painful way to cut spending. The stress was so intense that my body would shake uncontrollably and I felt like there was a huge weight on my chest.

It was in that time that God showed me that he would sustain me through prayer, friends, and fasting.

I committed myself to prayer and relied on the power of the Holy Spirit more than ever to get me through each day. I would labor in prayer and come away with a peace, which passed understanding. I praised God and found joy in His presence. The joy of the Lord was indeed my strength (Nehemiah 8:10).

God also surrounded me with good friends, great leaders, and the people I trusted most to provide support during this trying season. My wife, Pam, was my biggest supporter and confidant during the hardest days at Crossroads. She is a woman of strong faith. When I would convince myself the church was going to fail, she would force me to see the light at the end of the tunnel. When I was tempted to fall prey to negativity, she would instill words of faith. When I started to act in an unloving manner, she reminded me who Jesus had called me to be.

God also blessed me with two key additions to my staff: Mike Long, Executive Pastor and Taleah Murray, Executive Administrative Assistant. I had a long history with both Mike and Taleah and trusted them implicitly. Mike's knowledge and experience in church finance was going to be vital to our success. Taleah would be my representative to the staff and the church and I knew that she would represent me well and be the support I needed in order to be as effective as possible.

John Derry and Floyd Strater from Hope University took on a mentorship role and shared their wisdom born out of their experience in leadership. Larry Winger and Doug Crozier from Provision Ministries and Church Development Fund offered their advice and support. Sarah Sumner (author, speaker, and Dean of A.W. Tozer theological seminary) and her husband Jim came to my aid as well.

Peter McGowan, an Elder at Crossroads, not only provided emotional support, he offered the services of his design company, Plain Joe Studios, almost completely for free just because he loved the church so much. He called in as many favors as he could with his network of people to help us stay afloat and was a significant reason why we still had a quality service each weekend even though we had no money.

Every church leader should practice the spiritual discipline of fasting. It was vital in helping me stay focused on the Lord and His strength rather than my own during the tough times. Fasting gave me a new perspective on the situation at hand. When we fast, God does amazing things.

Then your light will break out like the dawn, And you recovery will speedily spring forth; And your righteou will go before you; The glory of the LORD will be your rear guard.

Then you will call, and the LORD will answer; You will cry, and He will say, 'Here I am.' If you remove the yoke from your midst, The pointing of the finger and speaking wickedness, And if you give yourself to the hungry And satisfy the desire of the afflicted, Then your light will rise in darkness And your gloom will become like midday.

And the LORD will continually guide you, And satisfy your desire in scorched places, And give strength to your bones; And you will be like a watered garden, And like a spring of water whose waters do not fail.

Those from among you will rebuild the ancient ruins; You will raise up the age-old foundations; And you will be called the repairer of the breach, The restorer of the streets in which to dwell. - **Isaiah 58:8-12**

During my first month at Crossroads, I was inundated with meeting requests. Some of these requests came from people in the congregation wanting to get to know me, some were unpaid vendors who wanted to yell at me, and some were developers who knew our situation and were vying for our land. When I got a call from the Mayor of Corona, I knew that his call was probably going to fall under the category of unhappy vendor.

You see, when Crossroads Church opened its Worship Center at this location prior to my arrival, it made an agreement with the city that within a year the church would complete the street improvements. The church is located on one of the busiest streets in the city and the sidewalk extended into the street in a very unsafe manner. On the corner of our property, in the middle of this protruding sidewalk, was a huge power pole which needed to be moved and would cost $750,000 to do so. The entire street improvement project would cost upwards of $2,000,000. I knew that this would be the subject of Mayor Eugene Montanez's meeting with me and I was not expecting him to be sympathetic to our dire financial situation.

I doused this meeting in prayer and asked God to give me favor with the city officials. Then, I took a deep breath and stepped into the conference room. Mayor Montanez, City Manager Beth Grove, and her assistant Brad Robbins greeted me cheerfully. Beth and Brad informed me that they had a wonderful history with my family here in Corona. My mother had welcomed Beth and made her feel at home on her first day working for the city many years prior. Brad told me that my father had given him his first job with the city. They both let me know that because of the impeccable character of my parents, they knew that they could trust me. Mayor Montanez let me know that he called this meeting to inform me the city had every intention of coming alongside the church and helping in whatever way possible. I left that meeting in awe of God and in love with this generous city.

The requests for meetings kept mounting and there was no way to keep up. One man in particular insisted on meeting with me, but my assistant was not able to get him on my calendar. He was determined. One Sunday, about one month into being the Senior Pastor at Crossroads, I felt a tap on my shoulder during the praise time of the service. I opened my eyes to see a hurting man who said that he needed to speak with me right away. Something in his countenance moved me to agree to meet with him at that moment and I ushered him into our Decision Room. I had no idea what this man was going to tell me, but I knew that I had to go out and preach a sermon in about five minutes so I hoped that he would be quick. The man wasted no time telling me that his wife was having an affair with our Pastor of Worship, the very man who was on stage at that moment leading our church in worship. There had been inklings of this pastor acting inappropriately before, but he had denied the accusations. However, this time I knew that this hurting man standing in front of me was telling the truth. As I looked through the glass doors at this worship pastor standing on the stage, the feeling of darkness that I felt on my first Sunday came over me. I went on to preach that day in spite of this curve ball I had just been thrown and I committed in my heart to pray about how God would have me handle this news. I asked Him to shine a light on this darkness if it was indeed true.

That week, I called this pastor into my office and let him know about the accusation and asked him to tell me the truth. He sat silent. I prayed. Finally, he spoke up and told me that the accusation was true. I proceeded to let him know that he was no longer on staff and that because of his prominent position in the church, I would be informing the congregation as instructed in 1 Timothy.

*"Do not receive an accusation against an elder except on the basis of two or three witnesses. Those who continue in sin, rebuke in the presence of all, so that the rest also will be fearful of sinning." - **1 Timothy 5:19-20***

I went on to tell him I would be willing to set up a restoration plan if he desired, because restoration should always be our goal as Christians. He broke down crying, overwhelmed by the consequences that this sin would bring. My heart broke as I thought about how this news would affect his wonderful wife and children.

I dreaded the upcoming weekend with every fiber of my being. This particular pastor was one of the most popular pastors on the staff. How would Crossroads react to his confession? How would they react to my decision to fire their beloved pastor? How much more bad news could the Crossroads family handle?

The answers to these questions did not matter at this point. God had called me here to do His work and to be obedient to His Word alone. I had to do what He required of me and trust Him with the outcome.

That Sunday evening, I held a congregational meeting with over 900 people in attendance. The sea of concerned faces stared at me in shock as I hit them with the news of their beloved pastor's infidelity. I went on to teach what the Bible says we are to do in such situations and let them know about the 2-year restoration plan that the fallen pastor would be going through. I finished my talk by reminding the church about the need for us to show forgiveness, grace, mercy, and love just like Christ had shown us.

When I had finished speaking, the worship pastor got up in front of the church and confessed his sin as his wife sat in the front row crying. In my mind, she was a hero. She stood by him and committed to do what the Lord required of her. In front of everyone, the pastor asked his family as well as the church body for forgiveness. The people applauded.

Because of the commitment I had made to God after the previous congregational meeting, I concluded the meeting by giving an invitation for anyone who wanted to accept Christ as his or her Savior. I stood in awe of God with tears streaming down my face as a flood of people responded to the invitation. The room erupted in applause, cheering for those who had found freedom in Christ. God took something tragic and made it into something beautiful.

*And we know that God causes all things to work together for good to those who love God, to those who are called according to His purpose. - **Romans 8:28***

Leadership Lesson:

Redemption and restoration is always the goal when a brother or sister in Christ falls prey to Satan's lies. God sent Jesus to save sinners.

1 Timothy 1:15 (NASB)
It is a trustworthy statement, deserving full acceptance, that Christ Jesus came into the world to save sinners, among whom I am foremost of all.

Paul knew this amazing grace, personally. He was once a raging enemy of the Church destroying families, forcing people to blaspheme Jesus, and condemning people to death (Acts 26:9-11). Then, Jesus came with grace and turned Saul the enemy into Paul the apostle. He was a new creation with a new calling.

David found God's restoration and redemption after committing adultery with Bathsheba and murdering her husband to cover up his sin. His crimes were heinous but God's amazing grace restored him.

Psalm 51:7-13 (NASB)
[7] Purify me with hyssop, and I shall be clean; Wash me, and I shall be whiter than snow. [8] Make me to hear joy and gladness, Let the bones which You have broken rejoice. [9] Hide Your face from my sins And blot out all my iniquities. [10] Create in me a clean heart, O God, And renew a steadfast spirit within me. [11] Do not cast me away from Your presence And do not take Your Holy Spirit from me. [12] Restore to me the joy of Your salvation And sustain me with a willing spirit. [13] Then I will teach transgressors Your ways, And sinners will be converted to You.

I love that the grace of God is greater than our sins and the blood of Christ more powerful than our iniquities. What a privilege it is that we get to be a part of seeing the lost saved and the prodigal restored. When church leaders lead out in restoring the fallen through love, truth, and transparency, God blesses the entire church. We need to do this for all people; not identifying anyone as being beyond the love and mercy of God.

Galatians 6:1-3 (NASB)

[1] Brethren, even if anyone is caught in any trespass, you who are spiritual, restore such a one in a spirit of gentleness; each one looking to yourself, so that you too will not be tempted. [2] Bear one another's burdens, and thereby fulfill the law of Christ. [3] For if anyone thinks he is something when he is nothing, he deceives himself.

Note: Paul says "if *anyone* is caught in any trespass." It is our duty to try to snatch every single person from the fires of hell. Our human nature makes this easier said than done, but praise God He did this for you and me.

A restoration process is a clearly defined path to bring about repentance and healing. It should involve a team of two or three spiritually mature individuals who will be actively involved in sharing life with this fallen brother or sister in Christ. Ideally, one person on the team is a licensed Christian counselor who will be able to identify the deeper issues and give this person the tools needed to overcome those issues.

Paul says that those involved in enacting the restoration process are to do so with a spirit of gentleness. The word gentleness comes from the Greek word, "prautes" which literally means "strength under control." In this case, it is the idea of being active in the restoration. The restoration team is to be gentle but firm in an effort to move the person from a state of brokenness to wholeness. The proper balance of reproof and kindness is crucial. Paul says they must do this while "looking unto themselves" so they will not be tempted. Jude warns that we are to reprove with mercy and yet with fear, "hating even the garment polluted by the flesh" (Jude 22-23).

A successful process of restoration showcases the beauty and wonder of the grace of God. However, it tends to be a long process of baby steps if it is done correctly. Remember, people are worth saving because Jesus died for them, and in the eyes of God, they are priceless. Not all restoration processes are successful. If people choose to stay in their sin, that is their choice. We must do our part and let them do theirs.

Chapter Four

Great Things are Coming

Call to Me and I will answer you, and I will tell you great and mighty things, which you do not know. **Jeremiah 33:3 (NASB)**

I wish I could say that this was the last of the bad news, but it was not. We discovered more unpaid bills taking our total up to $580,000. To add to the dismal financial picture, our cash reserves were quickly dwindling and there was no way to further cut spending. The next Sunday, I walked into the service feeling as though the church was not going to make it another week. I looked out at the joyful congregation gathering in the building and I realized how much I loved them. My heart broke as I pictured myself standing up on the stage the next Sunday to announce that we would be closing our doors. The music began to play signaling the start of the worship service and I closed my eyes to focus on the Lord and praise Him in spite of the circumstances. All of a sudden, I was overwhelmed by His presence and He spoke to me: "Great things are coming."

Call to Me and I will answer you, and I will tell you great and mighty things, which you do not know. - **Jeremiah 33:3**

Great Things Are Coming

At the Good Friday service the following week, God gave me a glimpse of those great things and my hope was restored. I am a creative guy by nature. I like to think outside of the box and illustrate my sermons in creative ways. The Good Friday services at CCV were "artsy" services filled with creative elements designed to draw people to the foot of the cross and identify with Jesus' suffering. I wanted so badly to bring that type of service here to Crossroads, but because we had no money, it just didn't seem to be possible. I brought our creative team together and we brainstormed inexpensive creative ideas that would emotionally connect people with Jesus' suffering. The team decided to build a huge wooden cross and have it lifted up onto the wall of the worship center during the service.

The next day, on my way to my office, I came across Cesar, who was building our huge, almost-free cross. He looked like he had been crying. I asked him how the project was coming along. He told me that in order to get the distressed look that we were going for, he had used a large, heavy chain to beat the cross. A few times, he took a blow to the back as he swung the chain over his shoulder. Through tears, he explained to me that the experience left a lasting impression on Him because he pictured what Jesus went through and understood His pain. That cross left a lasting impression on Cesar and it would leave a lasting impression on me as well.

On the night of the Good Friday service, I walked into a worship center filled with people passionately worshiping our King. As they watched the cross being raised and focused on Jesus' death, they cried. I sensed that God was taking us to a new level. He was uniting us and preparing us to overcome the obstacles in front of us, as long as we stayed focused on Him. At the end of the night, 15 people gave their lives to The Lord, and 26 people were baptized. This was the first time that I truly felt that I belonged at Crossroads. On Good Friday of 2007, we started on the road to victory.

The Day the IRS Showed Up

When you have $580,000 in unpaid bills, creditors call and threaten you, people want to meet with you to convince you to pay them, and the IRS storms into your office asking for your social security number and giving you the ultimatum of full payment or jail. Blake had discovered that we were behind on our taxes and had reported his findings to the IRS. Their response was to send an agent to our building with her badge out asking for our Social Security numbers in order to collect their money. I pictured them seizing all of our computers and freezing our personal bank accounts. What had I gotten myself into? Soon enough, everyone calmed down, and we did the only thing that we could do: handed them a check for the full amount and prayed for God to provide.

This blow took a physical toll on Blake. His hair began to fall out, and the heavy stress landed him in the hospital several times. He remained positive throughout it all, never letting anger and bitterness set in. But, walking a tight rope and uncovering obstacles that threaten your balance daily is bound to have some physical consequences.

I wanted to make sure that we were a church that accurately reflected Christ. To me this meant uncovering every penny that we owed, and paying our debts. During this process, Blake discovered a debt of

$100,000 that we owed to a man by the name of Brad Newell whose company had built the last phase of our building. I knew that we had probably cost this man a lot of hardship by not paying him and I felt compelled to contact him immediately to set up a meeting.

Brad exemplified Jesus from the moment I invited him to meet. He had heard about the precarious state of the church and offered to come out our way to make it more convenient for us! This was coming from a man who we had essentially robbed!

When we met, he genuinely wanted to know how we were holding up in the midst of all of the trials we were facing. The nicer he was, the worse I felt about not having paid him the money that we owed. I let him know how we had discovered that we owed him $100,000 and I sincerely apologized for not paying him when the payment was due and asked for his forgiveness. With tears in his eyes, he said, "That is all I need." He forgave us and said that we did not need to pay him, because he did not want to hurt the church. His heart moved me, but I let him know that we would pay him in full.

I went on to ask Brad why he had never sued us. After all it seemed like the logical thing to do. "Christians don't sue Christians," he told me. Later, I found out that he was advised by multiple people to take legal action against us, but he chose not to go against his convictions. I was overwhelmed by this man's integrity and faith; and I was determined to pay him in full. I had no idea how to make this happen, but God did.

Great Things are Coming

It was around this point in our journey that the economy began to go down hill. The Real Estate market was slowing drastically and the recession was looming. Crossroads' membership was made up of realtors, mortgage brokers, and people in new home construction who were not going to be able to give to the church like they once could, and there I was promising a man that the church was going to pay him $100,000 (not to mention all the other vendors to whom we owed a combined $480,000). The only logical place to go to make this happen was to our knees. We needed a miracle!

After much prayer, a plan began to take shape. The elders, staff, and I felt God leading us to enact a financial campaign to raise $580,000. We knew that the timing was terrible, and that this could cause us to lose the momentum that had just begun, but God was telling us to step out in faith.

The 40-day campaign was entitled The Dream Campaign. It challenged our people to give $580,000 in 40 days above and beyond their tithe. Crazy, right? But, our God does crazy things all the time! Parting the Red Sea was crazy, making people march around Jericho and shout was crazy, asking a lame man to get up and walk was crazy, and asking people to give an extravagant amount of money during a recession to pay off a church's unpaid bills was just as crazy.

We decided the best way to do this was to sell personalized glass blocks which would be placed around a lighted cross in the lobby of our church. The blocks could be personalized with pictures of loved ones, verses, or the names of the family. This turned out to be a beautiful scrapbook of the faithful people who sacrificed and came together to see our church set free from a mountain of bills.

After presenting the campaign to our people and making the "big ask," I felt like I was holding my breath until that first check came in designated for the Dream Campaign. The first check came in, followed by many others. People were giving. God was providing.

At the end of 40 days, more than $580,000 had been donated to the Dream Campaign! God was doing the great things He had told me about. We celebrated our freedom from financial bondage as a church family by shredding all of our paid off bills and shooting them out of confetti cannons as we worshiped the Lord in song. God had turned our mourning into dancing and He had bonded us as a church family.

One of the most significant moments that came out of the Dream Campaign was the Sunday that we presented a $100,000 check to Brad Newell in front of the whole church. This would be the first time Brad set foot on the property since completing the project. The Crossroads Worship Center building was originally supposed to be Brad's crown jewel because of the innovative architecture. However, because of how poorly he was treated by our church, the property instead was a source of hurt and pain for him. This day was going to change that perspective.

When he and his family showed up to church, I could see they were elated. At the end of the first service, I invited him up on the stage, apologized to him and his family on behalf of the church, thanked him for his grace, and handed him a check for $100,000. The church stood up and broke out in a thunderous applause. He and his family were overwhelmed with emotion. I found out later that God did something powerful in the Newell family that day. Not only did that moment signify

the darkness.

John 4:24 (NASB)
[24] *"God is spirit, and those who worship Him must worship in spirit and truth."*

When we lead truthfully and transparently, we gain peoples' trust and respect. They will follow because they know that we are for real and that we have nothing to hide. When a time comes for us to admit a fault, people are more apt to show mercy and grace. On the other hand, when we try to hide things, they eventually come into the light and those who follow us feel deceived and no longer trust the leader.

When we lead truthfully and transparently by God's wisdom, we win every time.

Chapter Five

Reaching the Next Generation

Let our sons in their youth be as grown-up plants, And our daughters as corner pillars fashioned as for a palace;" **Psalm 144:12 (NASB)**

Tony Wood

I am a Youth Minister at heart and although I was in the midst of getting the church through this crisis, it was killing me that we were not being effective in reaching the youth. So, you can imagine my excitement when Pastor Tony Wood, one of the best Youth Pastors I had ever trained, offered to come to Crossroads for no pay.

I met Tony when I was the Youth Pastor at CCV. We had 1,300 young adults in our ministry and God was doing great things at the church. It was after a night of worship that Tony walked up to me and asked if it was okay for him to be there. Feeling like there must be a lot to this question, I told him to come by my office the next day to meet with me.

The next day Tony came into my office and shared his story. His father was the Pastor of a mega church nearby. Tony had been on staff there as an Intern of Worship & Sports but had committed adultery with a woman who attended the church. When the affair was discovered, he broke his wife's heart by refusing to leave the other woman. Tony's father demanded that Tony work things out with his wife. Tony refused and withdrew his membership from his father's church. Everything about the situation was tragic. But, it had been about a year since the scandal and Tony had come to me repentant and ready to be restored.

I told him that it was ok for him to attend, but there were some conditions. He had to go through a time of true restoration process, which meant that he would end the romantic relationship with the girl with whom he had the affair, and he would seek to restore his relationship with his wife. He also needed to seek the forgiveness of his father and the church he had hurt. I asked Tony to attend faithfully for the next year and as I saw him progressing, I would allow him to begin serving and using his gifts. He agreed. This was not an easy process, but he followed through and we saw God move in incredible ways.

By the time the year was over, Tony had confessed and repented of his sin to his father and to the elder board of his previous church. They embraced and forgave him. Later, Tony would stand and preach in that church again and the people praised God because a prodigal son had come home.

Tony went from attending our church, to playing the guitar on our worship team. The more I got to pour into him the more I saw his giftedness. I asked him to speak one night for our college gathering and his talent and the way that God used him blew me away. Eventually, I brought him on staff to lead our next generation ministry. The ministry grew quickly in attendance and in depth.

Since I had come to Crossroads and was so overwhelmed with what we were dealing with, I had not talked to anyone from CCV. When I received a phone call from Tony and his wife Bre to meet with Pam and I, I was ecstatic to have a break from the issues we were facing at Crossroads and spend time with them. That night at dinner, Tony shocked me by telling me that he and Bre had been praying and felt God calling them to come on staff at Crossroads to start a young adult ministry. I laughed and informed him that we did not have any money to pay him. He told me that he was well aware of that and that he was willing to come for no pay. Their plan was to cash in his retirement and live off of that until we could afford to pay him. I could not believe my ears! He went on to tell that his father had given him his blessing to do this saying that God often called us to take huge steps of faith.

Pam and I sat there stunned. Tony and Breanne had children. This just seemed too much to ask. However, we needed them! We needed to reach the youth in our area. I advised him to talk to the elders at CCV and see what God would do. He talked to them, and they gave him their blessing. The transition began and I had no clue how big this hire would be for Crossroads.

Time for a Step of Faith

With the offerings being so low and Tony Wood's first day approaching, I was certain that Tony would have to live on his retirement. I let our elder board know about the agreement at the next board meeting and none of them liked the idea of someone with a family working for no pay and having no healthcare. We prayed and asked God to tell us how to proceed. When the time to vote came, the board unanimously voted to pay him no matter what. That next weekend our offerings went up, we had enough to cover Tony's pay and benefits.

Leadership Lesson:

One of the most important things I learned in this season is not to entrench yourself in and focus only on the problems. I am not advocating avoiding the problems, but I am saying that you must have vision while you deal with the problems. The Church has to continue to be the Church. We must exalt Christ, seek to reach the lost, help those in need, and be a true community. One battle I continually fought was with those who wanted us to do nothing else but pay down our enormous mortgage of $24,000,000. They reasoned that if we did that, we could eventually do great ministry. This is a wrong way of looking at things. I could not live with the thought of people going to hell while we did nothing. The area in which our church exists is a mission field. We found out that the Christian churches in our area were reaching only 13% of the population. My concern for the lost heightened when I discovered that there were over 40,000 young adults in our area and we were only reaching 200 of them.

There was no way we could live with ourselves if we focused only on our money problems and ceased to be the Church which seeks and saves the lost. Jesus did not say go into all the world and pay down debt!

Matthew 28:19-20 (NASB)
19 "Go therefore and make disciples of all the nations, baptizing them in the name of the Father and the Son and the Holy Spirit,
20 teaching them to observe all that I commanded you; and lo, I am with you always, even to the end of the age."

There is a fine balance that leading a church requires. We must be good stewards of our resources and be responsible to pay our bills, while seeking and saving the lost and making disciples. When confronted by those wanting us to only pay down our mortgage, I reminded them that God's blessing would only be upon us if we were an obedient church who practiced the great commission.

Good leaders must continually impart vision especially in the midst of crisis. Without vision people perish. During this season, I shared

n staff meetings, asking them to dream big and
e could reach more people for Christ. I also would
volunteers and most invested members regularly to
and let them know how important they were to
the vision God had for this church. I knew that the
t a big burden is with more people. Ten thousand
people could pay a $24,000,000 mortgage down faster than 3,000
people. Thus, casting vision allowed people to see above the
problem, as well as helped to solve the problem.

Generate

Tony Wood was a fireball of passion when he joined our staff. He hit the
ground running and his fervor was a magnet for influential gifted people.
One of those key people was Dan Pierce, who was a Varsity football
coach in the area. He came in as a volunteer to be Tony's right-hand
man. Together, they were a dynamic team of vision and implementation.
The mission field of students was white unto harvest and Tony and his
team were going to harvest in big way.

I started my ministry career as a youth pastor and spent 25 years of my
life ministering to young people. I love youth ministry and enjoy studying
each generation of young people and discovering what makes them tick.
The particular generation that we were trying to reach at this time was
the Millennial Generation, also referred to as Gen Y, the largest
generation by population next to the Baby Boomers. As Tony and I
studied this particular generation, we learned that they value spirituality,
heritage, family, and cause driven organizations. Instead of wanting to be
entertained, they want to be challenged to do something for a greater
purpose. The church is the answer to everything that they are looking
for, and yet we are failing to capture them. Studies show that this
generation is the least churched in American history. Tony, Dan and I
were determined to reach these young people and were willing to do
whatever it took to get them to Crossroads.

If we were going to be serious about bringing Gen Y into our church,
then we needed to make some serious changes. We decided to start
with our music. I was already making the shift from our worship being a
performance to a participatory experience, but now we needed to turn
up the volume and make it more contemporary. Now, if you are in church
leadership, you know that those are fighting words! People leave
churches over this issue all the time, but we were willing to lose some,

in order to gain a generation. So we went for it! And some people were angry. Some accused us of breaking the law, some left threatening voicemails for our sound guy, and some just shot evil stares in his direction during the entire worship set! Eventually, I had to make an announcement from the pulpit that the sound guy and the sound booth were off limits to the congregation. If they had a sound complaint, they could email me. But, the majority embraced the change, willing to give up their personal preferences in order to win the next generation to The Lord.

Next, we cancelled all "Sunday School" classes for young people that took place during the weekend worship services. I believe that it is counter productive to separate young people from the main worship experience on the weekends. If we separate them, then we tell them that we are not their church. If we incorporate them into our worship experience when they are in middle school, we will be more likely to keep them when they graduate from high school because they already feel a part of the main worship service.

Then we started a mid-week worship service specifically for young people. While we wanted our young adults actively involved in the weekend experience, we knew they needed a time which was focused directly on them and their needs. Months of preparation and recruitment went into the kick off of our Wednesday night Generate service. On December 5th, 2007 in our trendily decorated Worship Center lobby, 189 young people gathered together for our first Generate worship service. These young people were passionate, excited, and motivated to bring their friends. Each week Tony brought the Word, challenging this generation to be world changers for Christ and the attendance rose steadily.

The lobby filled up fast and they needed a new venue big enough to hold their growing numbers. However, the cost for the use of the worship center would be three times more than what they were bringing in their offerings. Money was tight still and we could not afford to have a midweek service in our main building.

As we prayed about what to do with our growing group of young people, we knew God wanted us to take this step of faith. We gave the green light for them to make the move into the main worship center and they were ecstatic! Instantly, their numbers rose to over 500 and through the next 2 years grew to 2,000.

In order to reach that many young people effectively, we had to put a lot of money into that area of ministry. We went from spending next to nothing for this ministry to having to spend 10% of our yearly budget on this ministry. God continued to provide.

Of the 2,000 who were attending Generate, many were from other churches and came because their respective churches did not offer a program for young people. About 50% attended the mid week service but did not consider themselves a part of Crossroads. This concerned some of our church leadership because they did not want it to become its own church and split off from us. I understood their concern, but surprisingly, I was open to them becoming their own church. If Crossroads could give birth to a church of 2,000 people, that would be awesome! I always let Tony know that I would support him and his team in whatever direction they felt God was leading them as long as he was truthful and honest with us and communicated through every aspect of the change. Tony assured me that he wanted Generate to continue to be a part of Crossroads.

I was so proud of the people of Crossroads and the changes that they had embraced in order to reach the next generation. Our church was now brimming with young people who were in love with Christ. Their passion was contagious and infused the entire congregation. We were growing and God was continuing to unveil the great and mighty things.

Chapter Six

Expanding our Tent

Enlarge the place of your tent; Stretch out the curtains of your dwellings, spare not; Lengthen your cords And strengthen your pegs. "For you will spread abroad to the right and to the left. And your descendants will possess nations And will resettle the desolate cities.
Isaiah 54:2-3 (NASB)

Kenya

There are times when God prompts you so clearly to get up and do something that it is impossible to ignore Him. This happened to Pam and I late one night while watching an episode of *Nightline.* The reporter was doing a story on AIDS orphans in Africa. I clearly remember two things that stood out to me. One was the response of the children when asked about their future. When the reporter asked the children what they wanted to be when they grew up, they answered with blank stares. Every child they asked responded in this same manner. They had no hope because disease or malnutrition was sure to kill them in their childhood. My heart ached as I watched these young children with no one to care for them and no hope. I looked over at my wife with tears streaming down her face and knew that God was calling us to take action.

The second thing that stood out to me was the fact that all of the children spoke English. If we went to help these orphans, there would be no language barrier. At the time, we were at CCV and we knew that God would not be pleased with a rich American church that let children starve. We knew that we could not help every orphan, but we could help some and that was what we were going to do.

Pam and I gathered a team, packed up, and left for Kenya to explore how our church could help. There were many heart wrenching moments on our trip, but one that is as clear in my mind as the day it took place was my encounter with a young 3 year-old boy. Our team was leaving a meeting with some Kenyan missionaries when a little boy who looked to be about three years old, carrying his baby sister on his back, came up to some members of our team holding out his hand. Both were in dirty tattered clothes and looked so hopeless. We had been advised not to give money to those who begged because then we would get bombarded with beggars, but we could not help ourselves. We gave the little boy some money and got in our van and began to drive away.

I asked our guide if he thought anyone was using these children to beg as a business. I had hoped that he would say yes because then I could have peace knowing that at least these kids had someone looking out for them. He stopped the van so that we could watch to see if the boy went to an adult somewhere to give them the money. The young boy carried his sister up some steps and sat down at the doorway of an abandoned building and opened his hand staring at the money in it. He had no idea what to do with the money. My heart broke and the urgency to do something to help these kids increased. God was calling Christians in the United States to be the answer to this little boy's prayers. We returned home and worked vigorously to start a successful ministry to these orphans in Kenya.

When I left CCV to go to Crossroads, I had made the agreement with the Crossroads elders that Crossroads would participate in this particular ministry. However, because of our financial problems we had been unable to put any money toward this ministry. But, I felt so strongly about God's calling for us to help these children that I had to make it happen.

Mike Long and I prayed and strategized about how to make this happen. We knew that God blesses churches that are generous just as he blesses generous individuals. We constantly challenge our church members to trust God with their finances by tithing. It was time for us to take that same step of faith. We decided to carve out 3% of the church's budget to dedicate to Global Outreach with the goal of getting to 10% as quickly as possible. We presented our proposal to the elders and they agreed. This was a huge step of faith because we did not have 3% to spare. Once again, God defied logic and provided for us.

Laguna Moment

Several months later, Crossroads was finally in a stable financial position and in a place where we were free to dream. I planned a retreat in Laguna Beach for our Elders and lead team to get away to pray, plan, and dream.

In one of our meetings, one of our Elders challenged us on only giving 3% of our offerings to Global Outreach. He asked why we had not yet moved to giving the full 10% like we had set out to do. I confidently let him know that we could not afford to give 10% at this moment. We were just now in a stable financial position and still had to be cautious with our spending. "Shouldn't we have faith, be obedient, and trust God to provide?" he replied. Didn't this man know that I was the Senior Pastor who had the ultimate faith and trust in God? Of course, I trusted God, but we had to exercise wisdom. Did he not realize that this decision would force me to lay off the staff? To my surprise, the rest of the Elders did not side with me! They unanimously agreed to raise our Global Outreach funds to 10% of our budget. I had been overruled. That night, I wrestled with the Lord. Anxiety crept in as I went through each of my beloved staff in my head trying to figure out whom I would be laying off in the next few months. I was like the Israelites who had a lack of faith even though they had seen God provide for them time and time again.

As it turns out, I didn't have to lay anyone off nor did I have to cut any spending. When I announced our increased commitment to the church, they responded by increasing their giving. God honored our obedience and provided in spite of my lack of faith. This was not one of my finer leadership moments, but I am thankful for God's grace and the leadership team that sharpened me during that time.

Next Steps

Over the next two years, we grew by more than one thousand people in attendance. God allowed us to do some great things over those two years such as being a big part of starting a rescue mission for the homeless, beginning an Adopt-a-Block ministry to serve the under-resourced people in our community, and baptizing thousands of people into Christ. Then, after those two years something terrible happened: our attendance stagnated. Then, something even worse happened: our attendance began to drop!

Now, I've been in ministry long enough to know that it has its seasons. Times of leveling off can sometimes be healthy because they allow a church to regroup and solidify its foundation. It's a time to evaluate and make necessary changes. The reason why I did not feel good about this season for us was because it seemed to last forever. Changes needed to be made, but I didn't know what to change.

I called out to God to show me why we were not growing and felt that He opened my eyes to what I like to call our "culture of poverty." Although all of our bills were paid, we were barely scraping by financially. In my mind, we were an awesome church who had been rescued from foreclosure just two years prior; in our church members' minds, we were a mega-church with a huge facility that could not get their act together. When you have a huge, beautiful facility like we do, people have certain expectations. Expectations such as a fast and efficient children's check-in system, clean and groomed grounds, speakers that work, microphones that are not being held together by tape, clear video projection, etc. When people looked around, they saw an impoverished church.

The only way I knew how to respond to all of this was to pray and fast.

Leadership Lesson:

Leaders should pray then plan. Fasting is an integral part of this. Fasting is one of the most joyous and intimate disciplines a Christian practices. When it is done correctly, amazing things occur. In Isaiah 58, God uses Isaiah to teach us the practice of fasting and the promises of fasting.

Isaiah 58:11 (NASB)
And the LORD will continually guide you, And satisfy your desire in scorched places, And give strength to your bones; And you will be like a watered garden, And like a spring of water whose waters do not fail.

When we fast, God promises to give us His guidance and to satisfy our desires in the scorched places. Our church was in a scorched place. The financial devastation that had occurred two years earlier made it difficult to operate in healthy ways. We were burdened with debt and felt like we were trying to swim in the ocean with weights tied to our ankles. While we were praising God we had survived, I wanted us to move past survival mode and into thriving mode.

Our Elders decided to spend the next 40 days fasting and praying for God to show us how to move forward as a church. We made a commitment that we would not make any plans or discuss any options until the 40 days had ended. We set a meeting at the end of the 40 days and vowed to decide our direction at that meeting even if it meant staying up all night! We had no idea what God had in store for us, but we knew that in fasting He promised to take us from scorched and dry to a well-watered garden.

I believe it is imperative that a Christian leader clearly understands the six aspects of Biblical fasting: Discipline, Focus, Celebration, Purpose, Generosity, Promise.

Discipline of Fasting

*"Why have we fasted and You do not see? Why have we humbled ourselves and You do not notice?" Behold, on the day of your fast you find your desire, And drive hard all your workers. Behold, you fast for contention and strife and to strike with a wicked fist. You do not fast like you do today to make your voice heard on high. - **Isaiah 58:3-4***

The people called out to God and asked why He had not heard their prayers while they fasted. God tells them that He has heard them but that He was not happy with how they were acting as they were fasting. They were using the fast as an excuse to be irritable and mean.

A friend of mine who is Islamic and lives in Israel told me that he hates it when Ramadan comes around in his town. Ramadan is the ninth month of the Islamic calendar and is marked by a month-long fast. The Muslims fast from food and drink from sun up to sun down every day and they feast at night. My friend said that he dreads this month because everyone is so irritable, unfriendly, and angry during that month and the whole town is affected!

We can be the same way if we are not careful. During a fast, you are to abstain from doing or eating something that is a regular part of your daily life. It should be something that hurts to give up so that you miss it often and when you do, you pray and connect with God instead. For this particular fast, I gave up sweets and carbs. As you can imagine, giving these things up can make a person quite irritable! I find that my sinful nature begins to manifest itself. I am impatient, cranky, and on edge. This is where discipline comes in. I must deny myself and choose to act in love instead of in anger. In fasting, we must discipline or train ourselves to act in righteousness and seek to be more like Christ.

*Then Jesus said to His disciples, "If anyone wishes to come after Me, he must deny himself, and take up his cross and follow Me." - **Matthew 16:24***

Fasting is beneficial because we practice denying self. In doing this, we grow closer to the Lord and more intimately connected to Him.

Focus of Fasting

In fasting, God wants us to pray more intentionally and intensely to overcome our lower nature and focus completely on Him. This is abiding with God. When we abide with Him, we become more loving like Him and His love is perfected in us.

We have come to know and have believed the love which God has for us. God is love, and the one who abides in love abides in God, and God abides in him. By this, love is perfected with us, so that we may have confidence in the day of judgment; because as He is, so also are we in this world. - 1 John 4:16-17

Jesus says that when we abide in Him, we will bear fruit and live a life that is effective.

Abide in Me, and I in you. As the branch cannot bear fruit of itself unless it abides in the vine, so neither can you unless you abide in Me. I am the vine, you are the branches; he who abides in Me and I in him, he bears much fruit, for apart from Me you can do nothing. - John 15:4-5

In fasting we focus on God and abide in Him by praying more intentionally and being more aware of His presence.

Celebration of Fasting

Isaiah points out to the people that God is not answering them because they are fasting as a means of mourning rather than fasting as a means of celebrating.

Is it a fast like this which I choose, a day for a man to humble himself? Is it for bowing one's head like a reed and for spreading out sackcloth and ashes as a bed? Will you call this a fast, even an acceptable day to the LORD?
- Isaiah 58:5

A time of fasting should be a time of celebration. We celebrate that we get to spend more intentional time with God and grow closer to Him. We should not walk around hanging our heads low, sulking in our misery and letting everyone know how miserable we are. Jesus reiterates this principle telling us to snap out of our self-pity and celebrate instead.

Whenever you fast, do not put on a gloomy face as the hypocrites do, for they neglect their appearance so that they will be noticed by men when they are fasting. Truly I say to you, they have their reward in full. But you, when you fast, anoint your head and wash your face so that your fasting will not be noticed by men, but by your Father who is in secret; and your Father who sees what is done in secret will reward you. - Matthew 6:16-18

We are to have a good attitude and celebrate the fact that we are fasting because being in the presence of God and abiding with Him is reason to celebrate.

The Purpose of the Fasting

Isaiah tells us that fasting brings freedom from the bondage of sin.

Is this not the fast which I choose, To loosen the bonds of wickedness, To undo the bands of the yoke, And to let the oppressed go free And break every yoke? - Isaiah 58:6

We are to see freedom from habits which are not holy or healthy. Fasting strengthens self-control, which is one of the fruits of the Spirit. In practicing self-control we overcome fleshly desires and instead pursue Godly desires. We find ourselves more aligned with Him and begin to pray for others to experience this same freedom from bondage and alignment with God.

Generosity of Fasting

Is it not to divide your bread with the hungry And bring the homeless poor into the house; When you see the naked, to cover him; And not to hide yourself from your own flesh?
- Isaiah 58:7

of our heart, mind and soul. We wanted to experience the blessing of obedience.

If you know these things, you are blessed if you do them.
- John 13:17

I let the elders know that this message would not be popular with everyone in our congregation. Some might even be enraged at the challenge and choose to leave and we had to be okay with that. Whenever you challenge the status quo, you will get resistance. I told them that I felt God telling me hundreds would leave the church, but thousands would come.

We knew that we needed to seek to please God and not man. After all that God had revealed to us, there was no other way to go. The vision that God had set before us was a call to complete faithfulness and obedience; the *Asah Shama*.

Chapter Seven

The Asah Shama

*... but so that the world may know that I love the Father,
I do exactly as the Father commanded Me. **John 14:31 (NASB)***

The Christian life is supposed to be one filled with love, infused with power, guarded by peace, and overflowing with joy because God is our Dad! Why does this not describe most Christians in the world today? I believe that it is because most Christians do not understand the significance of Exodus 24:7 and the truths therein. Understanding this passage is paramount to growth in the Church both in numbers and in spiritual depth.

For Crossroads Church, understanding this passage of Scripture sparked a revival. We crafted a two-year campaign around this verse and challenged our church to be a people of complete obedience. Although hundreds of people chose to leave the church, our church grew by thousands. People began experiencing God in a deeper way. Our church went from surviving to thriving. The offerings more than doubled over the next year and we were able to expand our Global Outreach impact beyond what we could imagine. Our people were finally tapping into the abundant life that Jesus promised us and it was all because we chose to be a people of the *Asah Shama*.

This campaign was so revolutionary for our church and such a pivotal moment in our church history that I feel a responsibility to share its components with as many people and churches as possible. Jesus did not live a boring, mediocre life and if we are to be like Him, then we are not to live boring, mediocre lives either! The truths that follow will radically change your life if you follow them. You will tune into the voice of God and He will reveal great and mighty things to you. Your life will be one of adventure and excitement if you choose to live according to these truths.

*Then he took the book of the covenant and read it in the hearing of the people; and they said, "All that the LORD has spoken we will do, and we will be obedient! - **Exodus 24:7***

Jewish Rabbis call this passage the "*Asah Shama*" based on these two Hebrew words in the passage translated here as "do" and "obedient." However, the actual translation of the word *Shama* is not "obedient," but rather "hear with understanding." I believe that is paramount that every Christian understands this verse correctly because it is life altering.

The children of Israel had just seen the glory of God and had heard His voice. Moses then comes down from the mountain and gives them the commandments he had received from God. This verse is their response to hearing those commandments, "All that the Lord has spoken, we will *Asah* (do with all our might) and we will *Shama* (hear with understanding)."

The Mishnah, also known as the "Oral Torah" is the first major written redaction of the Jewish oral traditions and the first major work of Rabbinic Judaism. The Mishnah's translation is based on the literal meaning of the actual Hebrew words used in the passage. Its translation of the phrase is, "All that the Lord says, we will *do* and we will *understand*."

The word *Asah* is translated into the English word, "do." In context of the word *Asah* means to "do with all your might," to do something completely. The Israelites emphatically stated that they would do ALL that the Lord commanded. It was a statement of full and complete obedience.

Shama literally means to "hear with understanding," to hear and perceive the meaning. This word is translated 785 times as "hear" in the Old Testament. The most famous place is in Deuteronomy 6:4 that is referred to as the "Shama" because it is the first word used in this passage.

Hear (Shama), O Israel! The LORD is our God, the LORD is one! You shall love the LORD your God with all your heart and with all your soul and with all your might."
                                    - Deuteronomy 6:4-5

In this passage, Moses uses the word *Shama* at the beginning to emphasize that they need to hear with understanding the command that he is giving them. In Exodus 24:7 the same translation should be used. The idea behind all of this is that faith grows when action is taken; obedience precedes understanding. This is a powerful concept that is life altering and paramount to our growth in Christ and to the growth of the Church.

This is a very practical truth with which most people would agree. Let's look at some practical examples. If you want to learn to swim, you could take instructional classes for weeks but you will not really learn to swim until you actually get in the water. You can watch YouTube videos on how to play guitar but you will not know how to play until you pick up a guitar and try. Instruction is great, but until we actually do something, we do not fully understand it.

This is true when it comes to our spirituality as well. To understand that there is joy in fasting, you must fast. The blessing of tithing will be foreign to you, until you tithe. The freedom that comes when you forgive your enemy will only be a nice thought until you actually forgive your enemy and experience that freedom. The same is true for intimacy with God. We cannot know true intimacy with God unless we are completely obedient to His commands. The *Asah Shama* begins with the phrase, "All the Lord has spoken, we will do." When we do ALL, we get ALL the promises and ALL the power of which the Bible speaks.

This is not a theology of doing works; it is a theology of loving God. Jesus tells us this in John.

If you love Me, you will keep My commandments.
- John 14:15

Jesus is clearly stating that the one who truly loves him will keep his commandments. We do not do this out of force but because we are compelled by love. We desire His will over our will. When we are in love with Him, we want to please Him and we completely trust Him.

When we do this, we are the recipients of two amazing promises. Look at John 14:21,

He who has My commandments and keeps them is the one who loves Me; and he who loves Me will be loved by My Father, and I will love him and will disclose Myself to him.
- John 14:21

Jesus promises that the Father will love us and that Jesus will disclose Himself to us. I want to expand on the second promise because it is so powerful!

The Greek word for disclose is "emphanizo," which literally means to exhibit, to declare, to manifest, to show. We get the English word "emphasize" from this word. Jesus is telling us that we will see His presence "emphasized" in our lives. Jesus is promising if we love Him and obey His commandments, He will clearly show Himself to us.

In John 17:3, we are told by Jesus that eternal life is to know God. The word "know" means "to know by experience." I can tell you that M&Ms taste incredible, but you will never "know by experience" until you taste them. Then, once you taste one, you will keep on eating them until you've eaten a whole bag of them. I can tell you that knowing Jesus is incredible, but you will not truly understand this until you experience Him for yourself. David tells us in Psalm 34:8 to taste and see that the Lord is good. In other words, "experience" His goodness. Once you do experience Him, you will want more of Him.

In Exodus 33, Moses is interacting with God face to face! Think about this. Moses and God were talking to each other the way you and your close friend talk over a cup of coffee or a round of golf! Moses knew God so well, that God allowed him to talk with Him face to face. In the midst of their conversation, Moses asks God for something remarkable.

Now therefore, I pray You, if I have found favor in Your sight, let me know Your ways that I may know You, so that I may find favor in Your sight. Consider too, that this nation is Your people. - **Exodus 33:13**

He asks for God to let him in on His ways so that he might know God better. He was already close enough to the Lord to have this type of intimate conversation with Him and yet it was not enough. He wanted more of Him. The more Moses experienced God, the more He loved God. The more he loved God, the more he wanted to experience Him.

Moses knew that by knowing the ways of God and living according to them, he would get to know God more intimately. In other words, Moses knew that if he loved God, he would obey His commandments and then God would reveal Himself by emphasizing His presence in Moses' life.

I have experienced this first hand. The more I spend time with the Lord and get to know Him, the more I want to know Him. Our relationship keeps getting better! I am more in love with the Lord today, than when I met Him nearly 40 years ago. I am closer to Him, more in tune with Him, and more aware of Him. Jesus has shown Himself to me.

Jesus' promise was true for Moses, true for David, true for me, and it is true for you if you love Him and obey all of His commandments.

What if you do not obey all of His commandments? Then, you will not know Him or be aware of His love. And you will miss out on the life He has for you. His power, presence, and blessings will be absent in your life.

Of course, we all fail at some point. We give in to temptation and fall short, but if your desire is to follow Him completely and your love for Him is real, then an occasional moment of weakness does not define you. Jesus is aware of our shortcomings and even sympathizes with us in them.

"For we do not have a high priest who cannot sympathize with our weaknesses, but One who has been tempted in all things as we are, yet without sin. Therefore let us draw near with confidence to the throne of grace, so that we may receive mercy and find grace to help in time of need."

- Hebrews 4:15-16

When we mess up, we are to draw near to Him in repentance and He will draw near to us. His grace abounds and His love covers our sin. Those who love Jesus find that He forgives, cleanses, redeems, and He restores.

In order to have an intimate relationship with Him, we need to be honest and transparent with Him. Jesus knows us better than we know ourselves and He loves us unconditionally. We must ask ourselves, "Whose will is supreme in my life?" Does your will trump God's will or does God's will always reign? Our will must be to do His will. This is what Jesus meant when He said, "Not my will, but Thy will be done (Matthew 26:39)." If our will is to do His will, then we will desire to obey all of His commandments.

Jesus continues in John 14 with another promise.

Jesus answered and said to him, 'If anyone loves Me, he will keep My word; and My Father will love him, and We will come to him and make Our abode with him. He who does

not love Me does not keep My words; and the word which you hear is not Mine, but the Father's who sent Me.'
- John 14:23-24

We see Jesus take this to a new level. Jesus says if we love Him and obey Him, He and the Father will make their abode with us. In John 15 we are told to abide in Jesus, but here, in this passage, we are told God will abide in us. The word "abode" is the Greek word, "meno" which means residence, dwelling place, or mansion. When we commit to doing all that the Lord says with all our might, we develop a deep abiding relationship with God.

With this type of relationship comes certainty. You know beyond a shadow of a doubt that God loves you and that you know Him. God wants this type of relationship with His children.

They will not teach again, each man his neighbor and each man his brother, saying, 'Know the LORD,' for they will all know Me, from the least of them to the greatest of them," declares the LORD, "for I will forgive their iniquity, and their sin I will remember no more. - Jeremiah 31:34

So the first part of living out Exodus 24:7 is to commit to obeying all that the Lord commands with all of our being and that obedience is compelled by love.

The next part of understanding this truth is to obey with all of our might. The concept behind the word "*Asah*" is to do with all your might. That is every day, in every aspect of my life, I live for Jesus and His will trumps my will. Paul says this should permeate our speech, actions and attitudes.

"Whatever you do in word or deed, do all in the name of the Lord Jesus, giving thanks through Him to God the Father."
- Colossians 3:17

Again, notice the word "all." God is completely committed to us and we need to be completely committed to Him. Jesus tells us in Matthew 12 that our speech reveals the content of our hearts. If someone loves something, that is what they will talk about. I have a friend who loves the Lakers and if I want to have an exciting conversation with him, all I have to do is bring up his favorite team. The same is true for people who truly love God. If we love Him, we will love talking about Him.

This is the biggest reason why Crossroads grew significantly during this campaign. Have you ever seen a house or car on fire? People flock to see what is burning. The same is true for Christians. When a Christian is on fire for the Lord, people cannot help but ask about what is so exciting. Our Church family was so in love with Jesus that they could not stop talking about Him. Their hearts were so overwhelmed with love for Him, that they could not help but talk about what He had done in their lives. They so easily shared their faith with others because their hearts were on fire for the Lord. They were lifting Jesus up and He was drawing people to Himself (John 12:32).

When our hearts are not filled with the love of God, it will be obvious by our speech. In Matthew 12, Jesus rebukes the Pharisees and warns them that their speech reveals their true character.

*You brood of vipers, how can you, being evil, speak what is good? For the mouth speaks out of that which fills the heart. The good man brings out of his good treasure what is good; and the evil man brings out of his evil treasure what is evil. But I tell you that every careless word that people speak, they shall give an accounting for it in the day of judgment. For by your words you will be justified, and by your words you will be condemned." - **Matthew 12:34-37**

Chapter Eight

Obedience Increases Faith

"The apostles said to the Lord, 'Increase our faith!'" **Luke 17:5 (NASB)**

Recently, I spoke at a church about how God does great and mighty things in our lives when we are obedient and have faith. After the service, there was a line of people wanting to talk to me about the things I shared. When Greg got to the front of the line, he very respectfully asked me if the God stories I had told in my sermon were true. They just seemed so unrealistic. I was assuring him that they were true and that God still does miracles, when the next man in line (who had obviously been eavesdropping) jumped into the conversation. Tom told Greg and I that the reason he was waiting in line was because he wanted to tell me that the exciting Christian life I had depicted was the kind of life he was living. As he lived a life tuned into God, great and mighty things happened all the time.

Many years prior, Tom had been challenged to obey the moving of God in His heart and mind. Tom believed in God but had never experienced God guiding him in a personal way. One day after reading his Bible, he asked God to speak to Him. This request was followed by a very random thought: "I should bring eggs to church tomorrow and give them away." It was a strange thought, but easily executed because Tom was an Egg Rancher. The more he prayed about this random thought, the stronger he felt about bringing eggs to church. So, he committed to take eggs to church.

The next morning he was already in his car when he remembered the eggs. He leaped out of the car with the motor still running and ran in the house to grab a few cartons of eggs. When his wife asked what he was doing, he told her, "God told me to give out eggs today at church." She gave him a should-I-be-worried-about-your-mental-health look, but decided that it really couldn't hurt to take eggs to church.

Once they arrived at church, Tom prayed for God to direct him to the person who was supposed to get the eggs. He saw a friend and offered him a carton of eggs, but his friend told him that he didn't eat eggs. Tom insisted that he take them, handed them to his friend, and walked into church. As Tom's friend was getting into his car to leave, a woman was getting out of a car right next to his. He greeted her and decided to off load the unwanted eggs on this woman. Her reaction scared him. She looked at him as though she had seen a ghost and then asked him if he knew who she was. He did not. She went on to tell him her story. She was a teacher at the local high school and was an atheist. Her students challenged her constantly on her atheism and she was tired of the debates. Her plan was to go to church today to prove God did not exist. Just before she got in her car, she set a challenge before God, "God if you are real, then I want you to have someone hand me a carton of eggs!"

Tom told Greg, that since that day, these types of miraculous occurrences happen on a regular basis in his life. When he committed to being completely obedient to God, his faith grew, and His relationship with God deepened.

Don't you want to live a life like Tom: a life full of miracles and God-stories? This is the type of life every Christian should be living. It's the life of ever increasing faith where we see mountains move and mulberry trees uprooted. This is what happens when you practice the *Asah Shama.*

In Luke 17, Jesus paints a picture of an extraordinary life. The apostles see that Jesus' faith causes Him to do miraculous things. They want what He's got and so they ask for it.

The apostles said to the Lord, 'Increase our faith!' And the Lord said, 'If you had faith like a mustard seed, you would say to this mulberry tree, 'Be uprooted and be planted in the sea'; and it would obey you.' - Luke 17:5-10

Jesus is telling them that people with faith like a mustard seed will see and experience great and mighty things. A mustard seed is very small. It is almost microscopic, but it gives birth to a huge plant that continues to spread itself and grow. I wanted to get one of these seeds and plant it to see what would happen, but when I mentioned this to someone who knew plants, they adamantly advised against it. They said that it would take over my entire backyard. I took his advice.

Faith like a mustard seed, is a faith that flourishes and overtakes every aspect of our lives. It is an obvious faith that flourishes regardless of the circumstances.

In addition to our faith being all encompassing, Jesus teaches that our faith grows in power. It goes from uprooting mulberry trees to moving mountains.

Then the disciples came to Jesus privately and said, 'Why could we not drive it out?' And He said to them, 'Because of the littleness of your faith; for truly I say to you, if you have faith the size of a mustard seed, you will say to this mountain, 'Move from here to there,' and it will move; and nothing will be impossible to you.' - **Matthew 17:19-20**

The Apostles had been faced with a demon that they were powerless against. Jesus enters into the situation and drives the demon out for them. They are confused as to why they could not do what He did and they ask Him to explain. He tells them that it was because of their lack of faith. When you have a faith that grows, you go from being able to uproot mulberry trees, to moving mountains, to finding that nothing is impossible. This type of faith leads to a life beyond description or imagination; a life of great and mighty things.

After Jesus describes this type of faith, He tells them how to get this type of faith.

Which of you, having a slave plowing or tending sheep, will say to him when he has come in from the field, 'Come immediately and sit down to eat'? But will he not say to him, 'Prepare something for me to eat, and properly clothe yourself and serve me while I eat and drink; and afterward you may eat and drink'? He does not thank the slave because he did the things which were commanded, does he? So you too, when you do all the things which are commanded you, say, 'We are unworthy slaves; we have done only that which we ought to have done.'

- Luke 17:7-10

Jesus tells a story of an obedient slave to illustrate how to have an ever increasing faith. The slave does what he is supposed to in the field. Then, after a long exhausting day of work in the field, he comes inside and does what he is supposed to do for his master. He is completely obedient and does what a slave is required to do which is tend to his master's needs and do as he commands. Notice in the last part of this section of Scripture where he says when we do "ALL" the things which God has commanded. This kind of faith only comes with complete obedience.

This is the same concept we find in Exodus 24:7. When we do all the Lord has commanded us to do, then we will understand the reasons behind those commands, and as a result, our faith will grow.

I heard a story recently of a couple that does missions work in Iran. They were traveling to the northern part of the country to give out Bibles to a house church. As they approached the town in which the church was located, the husband told his wife, "I know that you are going to find this difficult, but you cannot witness to anyone in this town." He explained to her the persecution and hatred for Christianity in that area. If she shared her faith, she would be putting herself as well as the house church in danger. She answered with silence.

They stopped in town and he ran to the bank while she went to the market to buy a dessert for the people of the church. When he came out of the bank, his stomach lurched. There, sitting at the entrance of the store was a Mullah, an Islamic holy man. If he found out that they were Christians, he had the authority to have them arrested.

With his heart pounding and his mind willing his body to stay calm, he walked toward the market. To his dismay, he heard his wife's voice passionately talking about Jesus! When he entered the store, he saw a small group of captivated people gathered around his wife who was animatedly sharing her faith. She was mid-sentence when he took her hand firmly and informed her that they needed to leave immediately. Disappointed and a little perturbed, she obeyed her husband and left the hungry crowd. They made it safely past the Mullah and into their car when she unleashed on him and reprimanded his rude interruption. Those people in the market needed Jesus and were hungry to hear about Him. The Holy Spirit did His work and convicted the husband's heart. He decided that those people's souls were more important than his safety. With an armload of Bibles and a resolute spirit, the couple marched back into the market. The crowd was still standing there discussing Jesus. The husband apologized to them and offered them the Bibles, which they gladly accepted, and invited them to the church.

As he walked out of the store, he felt the Spirit prompting him to give the Mullah a Bible. He thought, "If I am going down, I am going down big!" So he stopped in front of the holy man, looked him in the eye, and offered him a Bible. The Mullah gazed at the man in amazement and his eyes filled with tears. The night before, the holy man had a vivid dream in which Jesus appeared to him and told him to sit on a stool on front of the market where a man would give him the "Words of Life."

Crazy, right?! Not if you know the God of the Universe. If you are reading this and saying, "Nothing like this ever happens to me," I have a question for you: Why not? The Bible describes this kind of life. Jesus lived this kind of life. The apostles experienced this kind of life. And, Jesus promised this kind of life to those who are obedient and have faith. Jesus paid the ultimate price so you could be forgiven, know His love, and have life abundantly. Christians are given the Holy Spirit who reveals to us all the wonderful things God has for us, if we love Him and live our lives according to His purpose. Our lives then, should not be ordinary. They should be extraordinary; filled with great and mighty things. Stuff like this should happen to you all the time.

Chapter Nine

Doing Before Understanding

"Trust in the LORD with all your heart And do not lean on your own understanding." **Proverbs 3:5 (NASB)**

Really, God? For Her? But, she doesn't look like she needs me to buy her coffee. She is wearing a Rolex! She obviously has more than enough money and she's going to think I'm weird!

There I was, arguing with God in line at a bakery in New York. God had prompted me to pay for the lady in front of me, but it just didn't make sense to me. However, by the time she got to the cashier, God had won the argument. I leaned over and told the cashier, "I'll take care of her bill, just add it to mine." She turned and looked at me with wide eyes. *See Lord! I told you she would think I was a creep. This is about to get awkward.* To my surprise, she exclaimed, "Thank you so much! I love to bless people and do stuff like this all the time, and was just telling God that it would be nice to have someone bless me for once! And He sent you!"

What if I would have chosen in that moment to do what made sense to me? According to my human logic, this woman was nicely dressed, had no need for money, didn't look lonely and would probably think I was weird if I paid for her purchase. According to God's perspective, she was one of His beloved children whose prayers He'd heard and wanted to bless that day. Obedience precedes understanding. Why? Because we serve an omniscient God. God knows more than we do. He has a much broader perspective than we do. In fact, He knows the past, present and future. And, He knows us better than we know ourselves.

'For My thoughts are not your thoughts, Nor are your ways My ways,' declares the LORD. For as the heavens are higher than the earth, So are My ways higher than your ways And My thoughts than your thoughts. - **Isaiah 55:8-9**

God's understanding is beyond ours. His ways will not make sense to us at times because He has a higher perspective than we do. We need to trust Him and not rely on our own logic.

Trust in the LORD with all your heart And do not lean on your own understanding. In all your ways acknowledge Him, And He will make your paths straight. **- Proverbs 3:5-6**

Notice the word, "all." We are to trust Him with ALL our heart and acknowledge Him in ALL our ways. God requires total trust and total commitment. This passage goes on to warn against relying on our own wisdom.

Do not be wise in your own eyes; Fear the LORD and turn away from evil. It will be healing to your body and refreshment to your bones. **- Proverbs 3:7-8**

We do not know better than God so it behooves us to obey Him. When we rely on our own logic, we miss out on His power and the miracles that He wants to do in our lives. Too often, we rely on the gods of "I think" and "I feel" to guide us. However, God clearly tells us that we are to have no other gods before Him (Exodus 20:3). I cannot tell you how many times I've preached a sermon straight out of Scripture and had a line of people come up to me after the service to express their disapproval of my message because they "feel" or "think" differently than God's Word says.

A life guided by our thoughts and feelings is a dangerous life to live. How often do our thoughts and feelings end up being wrong? We are fallible in these two areas. There are many things that people throughout history have taught as facts and then discovered that they were wrong all along. This is why textbooks and encyclopedias need to be updated often. The more we learn, the more we discover how much we do not know. In Jeremiah 17, God warns us not to trust in man.

Thus says the LORD, 'Cursed is the man who trusts in mankind And makes flesh his strength, And whose heart turns away from the LORD. For he will be like a bush in the desert And will not see when prosperity comes, But will live in stony wastes in the wilderness, A land of salt without inhabitant. Blessed is the man who trusts in the LORD And whose trust is the LORD. For he will be like a tree planted by the water, That extends its roots by a stream And will not fear when the heat comes; But its leaves will be green, And it will not be anxious in a year of drought Nor cease to yield *fruit. The heart is more deceitful than all else Ana desperately sick; Who can understand it? - **Jerem***

Look at the contrast between trusting in man and trusting in Trusting in man leads to an unfulfilled life. Life lived trusting in God is a life with no anxiety that is constantly nourished and fulfilled. The picture painted here clearly illustrates how foolish it would be to trust in our own logic. Why would I want to rely on my humanness, when I can rely on an all-knowing God who knows better than me? We are a fickle people, but Jesus is the same yesterday, today, and forever (Hebrews 13:8).

In verse 9, God explicitly tells us that our feelings are deceitful. Have you ever felt like you were in love with someone and later found out you were very wrong? How often have you worried yourself sick only to discover that there was no true substance to the anxiety you were experiencing? We have no business relying on our own wisdom. Life lived by *Who* we know rather than by *what* we know is a life of obedience to God's Word. Our trust in God inspires obedience to Him even when it does not make sense to us. Then, after we obey, we get the understanding. Jesus describes this principle in John 8.

*So Jesus was saying to those Jews who had believed Him, "If you continue in My word, then you are truly disciples of Mine; and you will know the truth, and the truth will make you free. - **John 8:31-32***

Jesus uses the word "if," to begin this promise, which shows that we have a choice to make. We can choose to continue in His Word or not. Those who choose not to continue in His Word will not know the truth and will not experience freedom and will miss out on the presence and power of Jesus in their lives.

The next word that is significant in this passage is the word "continue." The word "continue" is the same Greek word "meno" that we looked at earlier for "abide." Remember, this word means "to live in" or "to dwell in." We are to live and breathe God's Word. In other words, it directs every aspect of our lives. This is contrary to living by the gods of "I think" and "I feel." It is the concept of doing with all your might even though it may not make sense; walking by faith and not by sight; trusting God with all of our heart.

The promise in this passage of Scripture is that we will know the truth and it will bring us freedom. Notice that the promise comes only if we oose to abide in His Word. First we obey His Word, then, through the obedience, we gain knowledge of the truth; by doing, we understand.

Let me give you an illustration of this concept. Let's go back to Proverbs 3. Remember, God tells us to trust Him with all of our hearts and lean on Him and not our own understanding. He then goes on to tell us to not be wise in our own eyes. We are not to reject His wisdom or His ways. I believe that what He puts next in that passage is a test of whether or not we will be found faithful. The majority of the people who call themselves Christians, do not pass this test. Look at Proverbs 3:9-12

*Honor the LORD from your wealth And from the first of all your produce; So your barns will be filled with plenty And your vats will overflow with new wine. My son, do not reject the discipline of the LORD Or loathe His reproof, For whom the LORD loves He reproves, Even as a father corrects the son in whom he delights. - **Proverbs 3:9-12***

"Honor the Lord from your wealth" means to give God an offering based on how He has blessed you. "The first of all your produce" is referring to the tithe. The tithe is the first ten percent of all income that comes into your life. I will dig into this command more later, but for now, ask yourself, "Am I passing this test?" Have you chosen to be obedient to this command from God's Word that asks you to give God a tithe and an offering?

This is a tough test. It requires us to trust God and not lean on our own understanding. It defies logic. God says here that we are to give money away so that we can have an abundance. Will obedience trump understanding? Do it with all your might, and then you will understand. Remember, God's perspective is much grander than ours. Trust and acknowledge Him in all your ways. Be obedient, then you will understand.

Chapter Ten

It's Not That Hard

For this commandment which I command you today is not too difficult for you, nor is it out of reach. **Deuteronomy 30 (NASB)**

I get the impression that many people feel like it is too hard to live this life of obedience. To live faithfully with and for God is just unattainable. Only the true "saints" can pull this off. If you are one of these people, I have some questions for you: Do you really believe that God has called us to live a life that is not possible for us to live? Is this incredible life of great and mighty things that He tells us about in His Word out of our reach?

Look at what God says in Isaiah 55:

*Ho! Every one who thirsts, come to the waters; And you who have no money come, buy and eat. Come, buy wine and milk Without money and without cost. Why do you spend money for what is not bread, And your wages for what does not satisfy? Listen carefully to Me, and eat what is good, And delight yourself in abundance. Incline your ear and come to Me. Listen, that you may live; And I will make an everlasting covenant with you, According to the faithful mercies shown to David." - **Isaiah 55:1-3**

The invitation is clearly for everyone if they choose it. When we come to faith in Christ, this life is the one He intends for us to live. God promises us a life of sustenance and celebration.

Milk is a reference to fulfillment. It is both nutritious and satisfying. The Christian life is one where God provides all that we need and we are content. When you are hungry and you eat a filling, nutritious meal, you savor each bite and when you are done, you feel satisfied. You do not crave other things because you ate just what you needed.

In this passage, wine is a reference to celebration. Wine was a luxury of life and a gift from God (Proverbs 21:17, Psalm 104:15). Wine was always

GREAT AND MIGHTY THINGS

a part of Jewish celebrations. When Jesus was at the wedding feast in Cana of Galilee, it was tragic when the wine had run out because it was such a vital part of the celebration. Here, in Isaiah, God is saying He will provide the wine. He is offering us joy and celebration. God is calling us to come and delight ourselves in abundance.

Moses' last words to the children of Israel was a plea for them to live the blessed life of obedience, and (since they were a people prone to negativity) he plainly tells them that it is not a life too difficult for them to live.

For this commandment which I command you today is not too difficult for you, nor is it out of reach. It is not in heaven, that you should say, 'Who will go up to heaven for us to get it for us and make us hear it, that we may observe it?' Nor is it beyond the sea, that you should say, 'Who will cross the sea for us to get it for us and make us hear it, that we may observe it?' But the word is very near you, in your mouth and in your heart, that you may observe it.

See, I have set before you today life and prosperity, and death and adversity; in that I command you today to love the LORD your God, to walk in His ways and to keep His commandments and His statutes and His judgments, that you may live and multiply, and that the LORD your God may bless you in the land where you are entering to possess it.

But if your heart turns away and you will not obey, but are drawn away and worship other gods and serve them, I declare to you today that you shall surely perish. You will not prolong your days in the land where you are crossing the Jordan to enter and possess it. I call heaven and earth to witness against you today, that I have set before you life and death, the blessing and the curse.

So choose life in order that you may live, you and your descendants, by loving the LORD your God, by obeying His voice, and by holding fast to Him; for this is your life and the length of your days, that you may live in the land which the LORD swore to your fathers, to Abraham, Isaac, and Jacob, to give them."

- Deuteronomy 30:11-20

One of my pet peeves is when people return from mission trips to third world countries and talk about how much better the faith of the people of those countries is. They seem to think that kind of faith is impossible unless you live in a third world country in extreme poverty. I love Global Outreach and I support short-term and long-term mission trips. I am encouraged by the faith of our brothers and sisters in Christ in third world countries. However, I do not think that we are excluded from experiencing that powerful Christian life because we do not live in extreme poverty. The life of passionate faith that they live is available to us as well. Moses says in this passage that we do not have to "cross the sea" to get this kind of life. In verse 14, it says that this life of abundance is so near you it is in your mouth and in your heart. Paul quotes this passage in Romans 10 and says that this faith in God is in our hearts and flowing out of our mouths. We have a choice to make. Will we choose to trust God, obey His commands, and live this extraordinary life? It's not a hard choice to make if you love Him.

The Power of Love

I saw a story on the news of a mother who heard a loud crash in her garage and ran out to see what had happened. Her heart sank at the sight of her college age son pinned underneath his car. He had been working underneath it and accidentally hit the car jack causing the car to collapse onto his body. Without even thinking, she ran over to the car and lifted it off of his body enabling him to crawl out from underneath it! The news reporter asked her how she accomplished such an impossible feat. "It was not that hard. It just happened before I knew it." Why was it not that hard for a petite woman to lift a huge, heavy car? Because, she was motivated by love.

I remember another news story I read while I was vacationing in Alaska. A polar bear leapt out of nowhere onto a man with his wife standing right next to him. Motivated by love, she rushed at the bear and beat it with her fists. The bear let go of the husband and ran away. An ordinary woman overpowers one of the most ferocious beasts on earth because she was empowered by love.

In the same way, if we love God, living a life of obedience is not that hard. As a matter of fact, it is not hard at all. It is pure joy because we are empowered by love.

For this is the love of God, that we keep His commandments; and His commandments are not burdensome." - 1 John 5:3

John echoes what he learned from Jesus. If we truly love God, we will keep His commandments and His commandments are not a burden to us.

I love my wife and it is not a burden to kiss her. Pam has an expectation that I will never leave the house without kissing her good-bye. I love this expectation! I get to kiss her every time I leave and she loves it! I don't ever walk up to her before I leave and say, "Do I have to kiss you again? This is really burdensome."

I also love my grandchildren. It is never a burden to spend time with them. At their young age, taking care of them requires a lot of energy and patience. They need me to make their food, get their toys, play dragons with them, change their diapers, watch the same cartoon over and over, etc. Still, I cannot wait to spend time with them and I get sad every time they leave.

The other reason it is not that hard to be obedient is because when we come to faith in Christ, we receive the Holy Spirit who strengthens and empowers us.

*For this reason I bow my knees before the Father, from whom every family in heaven and on earth derives its name, that He would grant you, according to the riches of His glory, to be strengthened with power through His Spirit in the inner man, so that Christ may dwell in your hearts through faith; and that you, being rooted and grounded in love, may be able to comprehend with all the saints what is the breadth and length and height and depth, and to know the love of Christ which surpasses knowledge, that you may be filled up to all the fullness of God. - **Ephesians 3:14-19**

This gift of the Holy Spirit is not earned; it is a gift from God. God freely shares His glorious riches with us when we come to Him in love. With His power upon us and within us, we find the strength to do what He asks us to do and to live the life He has for us to live. With His power, it is not that hard.

*For God has not given us a spirit of timidity, but of power and love and discipline. - **2 Timothy 1:7**

Paul tells Timothy that when we have God's Spirit, we are not timid or afraid. We do not have to fear failure. We do not have to worry about measuring up. We have power, love, and discipline (or self control) from God.

In Galatians 5:16, we learn that if we walk in the Spirit, we will not carry out the desires of the flesh. Instead we will produce the fruits of the Spirit: love, joy, peace, patience, kindness, goodness, and self-control. We only produce these fruits because of the Spirit's work in us, not by our effort.

Think about the significance of this. If the fruit of the Spirit is love and I do not love, then I am either quenching the Spirit or I do not have the Spirit. If the fruit of the Spirit is joy and I am not joyful, then I am either quenching the Spirit or I do not have Him. If the fruit of the Spirit is self-control and I am not disciplined, then I am either quenching the Spirit or I do not have Him. With the indwelling of the Holy Spirit and His power, it is not that hard to live the Christian life. It is not impossible to have the life of abundance.

I can do all things through Him who strengthens me.
- Philippians 4:13

Paul does not say that he can only do some things or only easy things, he says, "I can do ALL things," and he wrote this while in prison! This is true in the prison or in the palace; in times of prosperity or in poverty.

Jude tells us that this life of obedience is possible because God will use His power to make us successful in living it. Look at this promise:

Now to Him who is able to keep you from stumbling, and to make you stand in the presence of His glory blameless with great joy, To the only God our Savior, through Jesus Christ our Lord, be glory, majesty, dominion and authority, before all time and now and forever. Amen. - Jude 1:24-25

God is able to keep us from stumbling. He is able to make us stand up and stand out. He is able to keep us holy.

If you are still having a hard time believing that this extraordinary life is possible for you, then you must ask the question, "Am I truly in a personal relationship with Jesus?" Have you acknowledged Him as your

Savior and Lord? Paul tells us to test ourselves to see if we truly know Him.

Test yourselves to see if you are in the faith; examine yourselves! Or do you not recognize this about yourselves, that Jesus Christ is in you—unless indeed you fail the test?
- 2 Corinthians 13:5

Test yourself by answering this question: Is it burdensome for you to live in complete obedience to God? If we love Him, it is not that hard. If we believe in Him, it is not that hard. If we have the Holy Spirit, it is not that hard.

PART TWO

So, what are those commands that God wants us to obey that we might obtain His promises and live the abundant life? At Crossroads, we broke down the commands into the acronym I.T.E.L: Intentional Intimacy, Total Surrender, Experience More, and Love Like Jesus Loves.

In Revelation 12 we see a group of people who defeat the Devil.

Revelation 12:11 (NKJV)
¹¹ And they overcame him by the blood of the Lamb and by the word of their testimony, and they did not love their lives to the death.

One of the reasons they were victorious was because they had a testimony. They had lived lives of obedience to God and were testimonies of the truth of God's Word. God wants you to be a living testimony! If we practice I.T.E.L, we will have a story to tell and we will have a testimony. If you and I practice each of these, we will be aligned with God's will and will hear His voice when He speaks. We will be close to Him and He will tell us great and mighty things.

Chapter Eleven

Intentional Intimacy

*...but only one thing is necessary, for Mary has chosen the good part, which shall not be taken away from her. **Luke 10:42 (NASB)***

God has nothing better to do than to spend time with you! He longs to have a deep personal loving relationship with His children. If we want to take Him up on this type of relationship, we must be intentional about spending time with Him and abiding with Him. These types of relationships take work. If you want a great marriage, you need to be diligent about spending time with your spouse and communicating with each other. In the same way, daily quality time spent with God in His Word and in prayer leads to intimacy with Him. As we spend more time with Him, we bear much fruit, are transformed into His likeness, bring Him glory, and are aligned with His will.

John 15:1-11 (NASB)
[1] "I am the true vine, and My Father is the vinedresser. [2] Every branch in Me that does not bear fruit, He takes away; and every branch that bears fruit, He prunes it so that it may bear more fruit. [3] You are already clean because of the word which I have spoken to you. [4] Abide in Me, and I in you. As the branch cannot bear fruit of itself unless it abides in the vine, so neither can you unless you abide in Me.
[5] I am the vine, you are the branches; he who abides in Me and I in him, he bears much fruit, for apart from Me you can do nothing. [6] If anyone does not abide in Me, he is thrown away as a branch and dries up; and they gather them, and cast them into the fire and they are burned. [7] If you abide in Me, and My words abide in you, ask whatever you wish, and it will be done for you. [8] My Father is glorified by this, that you bear much fruit, and so prove to be My disciples.
[9] Just as the Father has loved Me, I have also loved you; abide in My love. [10] If you keep My commandments, you will abide in My love; just as I have kept My Father's commandments and abide in His love.
[11] These things I have spoken to you so that My joy may be in you, and that your joy may be made full."

Jesus tells us we will never experience the wonders and blessings of the Christian life apart from Him. In other words, we are not Christians without Christ. This seems so simple, yet so many people are missing out because they don't spend time with Him and He is absent from their lives. We need to be intentional about spending time with God daily. Look at the promise that verse 5 of this passage mentions when we abide in Him: "he bears much fruit." That means we will have:

- Hearts filled with love
- Overflowing joy
- Minds guarded by a peace which passes understanding
- Patience
- Kindness
- Goodness
- Gentleness
- Self-control

When we spend intentional quality time with Jesus, we begin to look more like Jesus. We do not work for these "fruits," instead He transforms our hearts as we focus on Him and learn from Him. When I was in Bible College, we had a professor whom all the students loved and admired. He was one of the best communicators I have ever known, full of passion and wisdom. When he got really excited about something he was communicating, he would stutter. We all seemed to listen closer when he did this. Before we knew it, we all noticed that we began to stutter when we got really excited about something! The more we were around him, the more we started to sound like him. Remember in John 8:31-32, we are told if we continue in His Word, we will truly be His disciples and we will know the truth and the truth will set us free. A disciple loves spending time with his teacher and becomes like his teacher.

2 Corinthians 3:17-18 (NASB)
[17] Now the Lord is the Spirit, and where the Spirit of the Lord is, there is liberty. [18] But we all, with unveiled face, beholding as in a mirror the glory of the Lord, are being transformed into the same image from glory to glory, just as from the Lord, the Spirit.

Paul tells us if we are where the Spirit of the Lord is, we will find freedom. Every morning I wake up, get my cup of coffee, and sit in my recliner with my Bible and meet with the Lord. Many days, I lose track of time because I enjoy meeting with Him so much. I don't do this every morning because I am forced to do it. I do it because I love meeting with Him and I find freedom in Him. Drawing close to Him daily transforms us into His image and this transformation brings Him glory. We become a reflection of Him in every area of our lives, and people see God in us and He is glorified.

In John 15:7, Jesus promises us that if we abide in Him and His words abide in us, He will answer our prayers. When we spend time with Him, we find ourselves aligned with Him and His will. His desires become our desires. Our prayers are answered and our needs are met.

1 John 5:14-15 (NASB)
[14] This is the confidence which we have before Him, that, if we ask anything according to His will, He hears us. [15] And if we know that He hears us in whatever we ask, we know that we have the requests which we have asked from Him.

John confidently made this statement because this had been His own experience. When we abide with Jesus, we are transformed into His image. We love the things He loves; seek the things He seeks; desire the things He desires. Our prayers become the prayers Jesus would pray in our situation. When we abide in Him, we are in His Word and His words are in us. He loves to spend time with His children. Make it a priority to meet with Him daily and discover the beauty of abiding in God.

When I first became a Christ follower, I didn't value spending time with the Lord. It was an inconsistent practice for me. However, as I got to know Him more, I enjoyed spending time with Him and disciplined myself to be in the Word five days a week for an hour a day. Then, when I transitioned into a Senior Pastor role, I realized that five days a week just wasn't enough. The enormous amount of stress that came with the position was shocking. I was busier than I had ever been before in my life and I needed more of Him to sustain me and lead me. I made a commitment to spend the first part of my day with Him every single day. I have not missed a day since I made that commitment and I do not know why I waited so long to make that a priority. Every morning, I look forward to meeting with God and hearing what He has to teach me that day.

In all honesty, it didn't start off that way. During the first one hundred straight days, there were many times in which I only met with Him out of duty, not because I wanted to meet with Him. Looking back now, I am so glad I forced myself to do it even though I didn't feel like it. I knew that if I allowed myself to miss a day, I would have made a habit of skipping my quiet times. After day 100, I obtained a new level of joy and intimacy with the Lord. I have not missed a day for more than 10 years. It is not a boring routine; instead it is the most exciting part of my day. I call to Him and He tells me great and mighty things I did not know.

HOW TO PRACTICE INTENTIONAL INTIMACY

First: Set an Appointment

Just as you would plan a meeting date, you need to plan a set time to meet with the Lord. This is the "Intentional" part. If you leave it to chance, it will never be a priority. Planning sets you up for success.

Proverbs 21:5 (ESV)
5 The plans of the diligent lead surely to abundance, but everyone who is hasty comes only to poverty.

Set a time to meet with the Lord daily and follow through. I prefer to spend the first part of my day with Him, but that does not work for everyone. Find the time of day that works for you and commit to spending that portion of your day with God.

Second: Start with Prayer

Start each session with a conversation with your Father in Heaven. There is no need to use pretentious language to try to impress God. Intimate relationships are relationships where you can be yourself, so be yourself when spending this time with Him. I like to take a walk and talk to God about the weather, or why my plants are not growing, or about my grandchildren. I talk to Him about my hopes and dreams. I talk to Him about what I am facing that day. At the end of this prayer time, free yourself from distractions and ask God to open your eyes to what He wants to teach you that day.

1 John 2:27 (ESV)
27 But the anointing that you received from him abides in you, and you have no need that anyone should teach you. But as his anointing teaches you about everything, and is true, and is no lie—just as it has taught you, abide in him.

God promises to use the Holy Spirit to teach you. This does not mean that we are not to have teachers. It is saying that we answer to God and Him only. While it is good to hear solid Bible teaching, ultimately we need to seek God and His Spirit to show us what is true. As you study, trust that He will guide and teach you.

Third: Have a Reading Plan

In the same way that you plan your appointment time with the Lord, you need to establish a Bible reading plan as well. A great way to start is to use the reading plan found in the back of this book. This reading plan takes you through the entire Old Testament once and the New Testament twice in one year.

After my prayer time, I make my way to my desk and get into the Word. I always have a reading plan which will systematically take me through the Bible. At this point, the conversation turns from what I want to talk about to what He wants me to know. I may read large portions of scripture (between 4 & 15 chapters) or I may dig in depth into one verse or passage that stands out to me.

Fourth: Practice the SOAP method

This is a structured method for you to get the most out of your time with God. SOAP stands for Scripture, Observation, Application, Prayer.

Scripture

You may be asking, "Which translation of the Bible should I read?" All of the different translations can benefit you in one way or another. The key is to know their purpose and what you should expect from each of them.

I would recommend that you read from one of the more literal translations. A literal translation aims to translate word for word from the original language. You can trust that the words used are close to the intended meaning. Some examples of a literal translation Bible are the New American Standard Bible, The English Standard Version, or the New King James Version.

Another type of Bible translation is a dynamic translation. A dynamic translation aims to translate the idea of the Scripture. This communicates the overall intention of the Scripture in an understandable way. The New Living Translation and the New International Version are examples of dynamic translations.

The Message by Eugene Peterson is a unique translation of the Bible which I enjoy reading as a companion to the literal translations. The Message is Peterson's one-man interpretation of the Bible in modern day language. It is useful when you view this as a commentary on the Bible.

Observation

After you read the Scripture, write down what you observed as you read. Depending on the amount of time you set aside, you can do this in a few minutes or a few hours. The point is to ask God to show you things as you read and write them down. This is a good time to write down questions and ask God to show you the answers.

Recently I was going through Galatians, Ephesians, Philippians, and Colossians during my meeting times with the Lord. I read a section each day. I observed that Paul repeatedly talks about our walk and how we are to walk. I noticed that people have to learn to walk. As a baby we reach a stage where we go from crawling to walking at the encouragement and teaching of our parents.

I watched a show once where models were being recruited and taught how to walk the runway. When they started, they had no clue how to walk the runway but after hours of training, I was amazed at the difference in their gait. The training of an expert made all the difference. In my journal, I wrote that I needed the Lord to teach me to walk so I would be one who walked in a manner worthy of the Lord and in the hope of my calling.

This took me on a journey over the course of the next few days. Here are my observations:

- We are to walk by the Spirit and we will not carry out the lust of the flesh (Gal. 5:16).
- We are to walk in the works God has prepared for us (Eph. 2:10).
- We are to walk in a manner worthy of our calling (Eph. 4:1; Col. 1:10; 1Thess. 2:12).
- We are to walk no longer as the Gentiles walk in the futility of their minds (Eph. 4:17).
- We are to walk in love (Eph. 5:2).
- We are to walk as children of the light (Eph. 5:8).
- We are to be careful to walk as the wise (Eph. 5:15).
- We are to walk in the manner we see in Paul (Phil. 3:17).

Then I came upon 1 Thessalonians 4:1 (NASB),

[1] *Finally then, brethren, we request and exhort you in the Lord Jesus, that as you received from us instruction as to how you ought to walk and please God (just as you actually do walk),that you excel still more.*

I observed that Paul says he gave us instructions on how we are to "walk." I went back through my observations and underneath each one, I wrote out how they could be applied to my life, which leads us into the next step.

Application

After you have read and written down your observations, you need to apply it to your life. Ask God to show you how this truth applies to your life. In my study on walking, I went back through each of my observations and wrote out practical applications for my life. I learned that I am called to study, preach, teach, lead and care for those who are in the Church. I am called to seek and save the lost. I am called by God to care for the hurting and those in need. I am called to mentor leaders and equip leaders to use their gifts.

Prayer

Write down a prayer to God in light of what He taught you that day. When you take the time to write the prayer out, it slows you down and causes you to tune into God. Many times, when I am writing out my prayer, I hear or sense Him talking to me. There have been many times when I have sensed the Lord telling me to pray differently; sometimes He asks me to pray bigger!

Written down prayers also serve as a reminder of God's faithfulness. You can look back at your prayers and see how God has answered. To get ready for this book, I went through some of my journals from six years ago. I was awed by the way He answered my prayers in my most desperate moments. Because I had written my prayers down, I was reminded of the amazing things God had done.

The more intentional time you spend with the Lord, the more you will be tuned into His voice. I like to think of it as tuning into a radio station. Right now as you are reading this, there is someone singing, someone laughing, someone crying, someone talking. The way to hear all of these people is to tune into the right radio station. The airwaves are filled with these sounds at all times, but we can only hear them if we turn on the radio and tune into the correct station. God is always speaking. We need to tune in to hear what He is saying to us. Job 33:14 tells us that often God speaks, but no one notices. Choose to be someone who hears

Him when He speaks. Be intentional about tuning into Him daily and experience the promise of Jeremiah 33:3 (NASB),

[3] 'Call to Me and I will answer you, and I will tell you great and mighty things, which you do not know.'

Chapter Twelve

Total Surrender

"Why do you call Me, 'Lord, Lord,' and do not do what I say?"
Luke 6:46 (NASB)

My wife Pam went sky diving once. I told her that she was crazy and then took out a huge life insurance policy on her, prior to her dive. The thought of jumping out of a plane from over 12,000 feet up in the air to free fall at 115 mph while completely trusting someone I just met to pull a chute open gives me anxiety! If you've ever been sky diving, you know that usually you must skydive in tandem with an expert sky diver who does all of the work to pull the parachute open and land you safely on the ground. Once you throw yourself out of that plane, your life is completely in this expert's hands. You do what he tells you to do and trust him to do his job. You also trust that the equipment will function the way it is supposed to function and that it was properly set up. According to Pam, the experience of free falling and surrendering all control to the expert is exhilarating.

Life with God is meant to be exhilarating. But, we can only experience this exhilaration if we totally surrender our time, talent, and treasure to the expert and do what He tells us to do with those gifts that He has given us.

A man set out on a solo hike to enjoy nature and draw closer to God. He had reached the top of a majestic mountain and was standing on the edge amazed at the valley before him. Suddenly, the ground gave way and he began plummeting down into the valley. He frantically grabbed at the dirt trying to grasp a hold of something that might save his life. Finally, he caught the small branches of a tree protruding from the mountainside. Dangling in mid air, he could feel his hands slipping from the muddy branches. He yelled, "Is there anyone up there who can help me?" Only the sound of his own voice echoed back. Then, he cried out, "Oh, please God, help me!" To his surprise, a voice out of nowhere responded, "I will." He gasped, "God is that you?" God replied, "Yes, it is Me and I will help you. Just let go of the branch." The man answered, "Is there anyone else up there who can help me?"

God asks for a TOTAL surrender of our lives. As the old saying goes, "If He is not Lord of all, then He is not Lord at all." We cannot only trust Him with some areas of our lives and expect to live the abundant life, because a half-hearted commitment to God buys you a subpar life devoid of power. God desires hearts totally surrendered to Him willing to do whatever He asks.

Luke 9:62 (NASB)
62 But Jesus said to him, "No one, after putting his hand to the plow and looking back, is fit for the kingdom of God."

Mark 10:28-30 (NASB)
28 Peter began to say to Him, "Behold, we have left everything and followed You." 29 Jesus said, "Truly I say to you, there is no one who has left house or brothers or sisters or mother or father or children or farms, for My sake and for the gospel's sake, 30 but that he will receive a hundred times as much now in the present age, houses and brothers and sisters and mothers and children and farms, along with persecutions; and in the age to come, eternal life.

James 1:6-8 (NASB)
6 But he must ask in faith without any doubting, for the one who doubts is like the surf of the sea, driven and tossed by the wind.
7 For that man ought not to expect that he will receive anything from the Lord, 8 being a double-minded man, unstable in all his ways.

Revelation 3:15-16 (NASB)
15 'I know your deeds, that you are neither cold nor hot; I wish that you were cold or hot. 16 'So because you are lukewarm, and neither hot nor cold, I will spit you out of My mouth.

Obedience in the areas of our time, talent, and treasure requires us to let go and completely trust God. Much of what He asks will not make sense to our human minds but we must remember that His thoughts are higher than ours and He knows what is best for us. He is our Father who likes to give good gifts to His children.

Hebrews 11:6 (NASB)
6 And without faith it is impossible to please Him, for he who comes to God must believe that He is and that He is a rewarder of those who seek Him.

James 1:17 (NASB)
[17] *Every good thing given and every perfect gift is from above, coming down from the Father of lights, with whom there is no variation or shifting shadow.*

We are in good hands when we entrust ourselves completely to God. We can jump out of the plane and let go of the branch knowing that our Father in Heaven will take us to new heights. Are you willing to surrender all and do all that He asks of you when it comes to your time, talent, and treasure?

Time & Talent

Each of us has a unique calling, purpose, and destiny for our lives. However, we are all called to be like Christ and Christ was a servant. We will find our unique God-ordained destiny only by using our time and talent to serve God and serve others.

Romans 8:28-30 (NASB)
[28] *And we know that God causes all things to work together for good to those who love God, to those who are called according to His purpose.* [29] *For those whom He foreknew, He also predestined to become conformed to the image of His Son, so that He would be the firstborn among many brethren;* [30] *and these whom He predestined, He also called; and these whom He called, He also justified; and these whom He justified, He also glorified.*

We must love God and live out His purpose for our lives in order to receive the promise of Him working all things together for our good. Living out His purpose is being conformed to the image of Christ. The only way to do this is to be disciples of Jesus. A disciple learns from his master with the goal of becoming like his master.

Matthew 10:24-25 (NASB)
[24] *"A disciple is not above his teacher, nor a slave above his master.* [25] *It is enough for the disciple that he become like his teacher, and the slave like his master."*

He must be our Lord, which means He has complete authority over us dictating our every move, and we need to strive to imitate Him. What did Jesus do? He served and He told us to do the same.

John 13:12-17 (NASB)

^{12} So when He had washed their feet, and taken His garments and reclined at the table again, He said to them, "Do you know what I have done to you? ^{13} You call Me Teacher and Lord; and you are right, for so I am. ^{14} If I then, the Lord and the Teacher, washed your feet, you also ought to wash one another's feet. ^{15} For I gave you an example that you also should do as I did to you. ^{16} Truly, truly, I say to you, a slave is not greater than his master, nor is one who is sent greater than the one who sent him. ^{17} If you know these things, you are blessed if you do them."

Matthew 23:11 (NASB)

^{11} "But the greatest among you shall be your servant."

Are you serving Him? How are you using your time and talents to serve the body of Christ? Jesus says that we are blessed if we *do* what His Word tells us to do, not if we just *know* what His Word says. Jesus gave you a spiritual gift (a talent) for you to be able to serve Him in a significant way. God has prepared good works for you to do. Are you doing them?

Ephesians 2:10 (NASB)

^{10} For we are His workmanship, created in Christ Jesus for good works, which God prepared beforehand so that we would walk in them.

A faithful servant surrenders their time and talent to their master. If we are truly disciples of Christ and desire to live the abundant life and discover our destiny, then we must surrender our time and talents to God by using them for His glory. Obedience is imperative!

I heard the story of a son who asked his father for a car. He told his father that it would make life better not only for himself, but also for his parents. They would not have to be his personal taxi anymore allowing them more freedom. His father said he would pray and think about it.

A week later, the father handed his son a book. He told the son that he really wanted him to read the book, and when he finished it he wanted to discuss it with him. The son replied, "Have you thought about buying me a car?" The father answered, "Read the book and we will discuss that later."

Over the next month, the son came to his father multiple times asking about the car. Each time, his father asked him to read the book. For three months this continued. Finally, the son relented and read the book. When he came to the last chapter, he turned the page and saw his father's handwriting. The note said, "Son, your mother and I do believe you should have your own car. When you finish reading this, come to me and I will give you the keys." Elated, the son ran to his father. The father let him know that the car had been in his uncles' garage for the past three months waiting for him. The gift was waiting for him and all he had to do was be obedient.

God wants to give us good gifts. He wants to bless us and show us things that are beyond description and imagination. When we are obedient, we receive these blessings.

The number one excuse I hear for people not being faithful in this area is, "I don't have time." My response to that is, "Liar!" God has given you all the time you need and He asked you to use this gift of time that He has given you to serve Him. Are you using your time to build up the body of Christ, or are you using your time for selfish pleasures?

Jesus clearly talks about the consequences of using our time unwisely in the Parable of the Talents. I encourage you not to skim over this parable. Read it carefully and pay attention to what Jesus is saying. I want to warn you ahead of time not to play mental olympics with verse 30. Jesus means what he says.

Matthew 25:14-30 (NASB)
[14] "For it is just like a man about to go on a journey, who called his own slaves and entrusted his possessions to them. [15] To one he gave five talents, to another, two, and to another, one, each according to his own ability; and he went on his journey.
[16] Immediately the one who had received the five talents went and traded with them, and gained five more talents. [17] In the same manner the one who had received the two talents gained two more. [18] But he who received the one talent went away, and dug a hole in the ground and hid his master's money.
[19] Now after a long time the master of those slaves *came and *settled accounts with them. [20] The one who had received the five talents came up and brought five more talents, saying, 'Master, you entrusted five talents to me. See, I have gained five more talents.' [21] His master said to him, 'Well done, good and faithful slave. You were faithful with a few things, I will put you in charge of many things; enter into the joy of your master.'
[22] "Also the one who had received the two talents came up and said, 'Master, you entrusted two talents to me. See, I have gained two more talents.' [23] His master said to him, 'Well done, good and faithful slave.

You were faithful with a few things, I will put you in charge of many things; enter into the joy of your master.'
[24] And the one also who had received the one talent came up and said, 'Master, I knew you to be a hard man, reaping where you did not sow and gathering where you scattered no seed. [25] And I was afraid, and went away and hid your talent in the ground. See, you have what is yours.'
[26] But his master answered and said to him, 'You wicked, lazy slave, you knew that I reap where I did not sow and gather where I scattered no seed. [27] Then you ought to have put my money in the bank, and on my arrival I would have received my money back with interest. [28] Therefore take away the talent from him, and give it to the one who has the ten talents.' [29] For to everyone who has, more shall be given, and he will have an abundance; but from the one who does not have, even what he does have shall be taken away. [30] Throw out the worthless slave into the outer darkness; in that place there will be weeping and gnashing of teeth."

When Jesus comes to settle accounts with you and I, will we be found faithful? Jesus pours out a rich blessing on the faithful slave, but the unfaithful slave He casts into Hell.

This is the consequence for disobedience. This is the judgment that comes upon the one who says he or she is a Christian and yet does nothing. I am not saying that we are saved by what we do. We are saved by grace, not works. However, one who has experienced God's grace will do what God says and God says to serve Him.

In a parallel account of this parable, Luke brings out a very important truth:

Luke 19:17 (NASB)
[17] And he said to him, "Well done, good slave, because you have been faithful in a very little thing, you are to be in authority over ten cities."

Are we faithful even when it comes to the "little" or "small" thing? Jesus does not miss the "little" things we do. In the eyes of God there are no small acts of kindness or service. One of my favorite passages of scripture is Zechariah 4:10 (NASB),

[10] For who has despised the day of small things? But these seven will be glad when they see the plumb line in the hand of Zerubbabel—these are the eyes of the LORD which range to and fro throughout the earth.

God had Zechariah bring this message to people who were serving God and being told that their acts of service did not matter because the acts were not big enough or good enough. God declares that their service is not a small thing to Him. Any service we do for Him and in His name matters.

We just need to be obedient and serve Him in whatever way we can and then watch what God does with it. Pam and I befriended a wonderful couple in our church who wanted to find a place to serve. When the husband heard that we needed people to prepare the communion elements, he volunteered immediately. This may be looked at as a small thing that has no significance, but the couple was faithful and served God in this way.

Eventually they led the communion preparation ministry because they were so faithful, and I referred a young couple to that ministry who had just become engaged. This young couple built a close relationship with the older couple as they served side by side. After the young couple got married, they hit a rough patch in their marriage and were so unhappy and miserable. One day while preparing communion together, the young couple shared their struggles with the older couple. The older couple was able to mentor and pray this young couple through this rough patch and help strengthen their marriage. Saving a marriage is not a "small" thing. God saw that this older couple was faithful in the "little" things and entrusted them with a "big" thing. Be obedient and use your time and talent to serve Him.

King Asa in the book of 2 Chronicles is a King who missed out on the blessings of God because instead of being obedient to God, he trusted in man. Listen to God's response to the King's unfaithful heart.

2 Chronicles 16:9 (NASB)
⁹ "For the eyes of the LORD move to and fro throughout the earth that He may strongly support those whose heart is completely His. You have acted foolishly in this. Indeed, from now on you will surely have wars."

When you read the context of this Scripture, you see that his disobedience not only affected him, it affected the lives of many others as well. When we are faithful to God by totally surrendering our time, talent and treasure we get blessed and others get blessed. If we are not faithful, we miss out on the blessing of God and others miss out as well.

God has given you a spiritual gift (talent). Paul tells us we are to use the gifts we have according to the grace God has given us.

Romans 12:6-8 (NASB)

⁶ Since we have gifts that differ according to the grace given to us, each of us is to exercise them accordingly: if prophecy, according to the proportion of his faith; ⁷ if service, in his serving; or he who teaches, in his teaching; ⁸ or he who exhorts, in his exhortation; he who gives, with liberality; he who leads, with diligence; he who shows mercy, with cheerfulness.

It is vital that each one of us use our gifts to serve the Lord. Picture the church as a puzzle and each person is a piece of the puzzle. When they use their gift to serve the church, their puzzle piece is put into place. However, if they choose not to use their gift, the piece will always be missing and it's noticeable and affects the entire puzzle in a negative way because it's a missing piece!

There is a story told of Satan calling a meeting in hell. The Church was moving forward and the gates of hell were not prevailing. He needed a strategy to stop the Church and make it ineffective. One of his demons proposed they spread the lie that God is not real. Satan said they would do that, but that would not be enough. Another demon spoke up and said they should spread the lie that hell did not exist. Satan said that while that was a great idea, it wouldn't be enough. Then, his most evil and vicious demon came up with the strategy that made all the demons of hell cheer; they would spread the lie, "There is no hurry."

We need to be a people of urgency. God has work for us to do, so let's be like the faithful servant and make the most of our time here.

Jeremiah 29:11-13 (NASB)

¹¹ 'For I know the plans that I have for you,' declares the LORD, 'plans for welfare and not for calamity to give you a future and a hope. ¹² Then you will call upon Me and come and pray to Me, and I will listen to you. ¹³ You will seek Me and find Me when you search for Me with all your heart.'

God has a plan for your life, a unique destiny that He has designed for you. His plans are for your good. He wants the best for you. He has asked you to use your time and talent to serve the Kingdom of God. Will you choose to be obedient?

Chapter Thirteen

Total Surrender, A Matter of the Heart

'This people honors me with their lips, but their heart is far away from me.' **Matthew 15:8 (NASB)**

Treasure

Whenever money is talked about from the pulpit, people tend to get uncomfortable. I notice that people find their sermon notes really interesting on the days I talk about money, because they refuse to make eye contact with me! God clearly tells us in His Word that our first fruits, the first 10% of all of our income, belong to Him and that in addition to that we are to give offerings. Yet, so many Christians fight this and create theological arguments to get out of it. They have chosen not to practice the *Asah Shama* and are missing out on the abundant life. Why is it that we get so offended at God for asking us to return back to Him a portion of what He has blessed us with? Perhaps it's all part of Satan's plan.

Jesus warned us about the enemy who comes to rob us of the abundant life (John 10:10). This has been true since man's beginning. Satan slithered through the Garden of Eden with a sinister plan to ruin Adam and Eve's blessed life. He got to Eve by questioning God's integrity.

Genesis 3:1-4 (NASB)
¹ Now the serpent was more crafty than any beast of the field which the LORD God had made. And he said to the woman, "Indeed, has God said, 'You shall not eat from any tree of the garden'?" ² The woman said to the serpent, "From the fruit of the trees of the garden we may eat; ³ but from the fruit of the tree which is in the middle of the garden, God has said, 'You shall not eat from it or touch it, or you will die.'" ⁴ The serpent said to the woman, "You surely will not die!"

Satan uses this same strategy, trying to derail God's plans for Jesus when he is tempting Him in the desert. In Matthew 4 and Luke 4 we see

Satan question "if" Jesus really is the Son of God. Satan even quotes Scripture and tries to get Jesus to worship him instead of worshipping God. Today, Satan is up to his same old tricks, trying to rob you of the blessings God has for you and attempting to destroy you.

2 Corinthians 10:3-6 (NASB)
³ For though we walk in the flesh, we do not war according to the flesh, ⁴ for the weapons of our warfare are not of the flesh, but divinely powerful for the destruction of fortresses. ⁵ We are destroying speculations and every lofty thing raised up against the knowledge of God, and we are taking every thought captive to the obedience of Christ, ⁶ and we are ready to punish all disobedience, whenever your obedience is complete.

We need to beware of our enemy's plot to get us to speculate; questioning God's commands and promoting disobedience. Unfortunately, Satan is quite successful with Christians in promoting disobedience in the area of finances. He has convinced many Christians that God is a liar.

Matthew 6:24 (NKJV)
²⁴ "No one can serve two masters; for either he will hate the one and love the other, or else he will be loyal to the one and despise the other. You cannot serve God and mammon."

Some English translations of the Bible use the word "wealth" for the word "mammon." Jesus spoke in Aramaic and the word he used is "mammon." While this word does refer to wealth, it seems to have a deeper meaning. According to Easton's Bible Dictionary and Holman Illustrated Bible, "Mammon" is a reference to a false God. Thomas Aquinas says that he saw "Mammon being carried up from Hell by a wolf, coming to inflame the human heart with greed." Milton in *Paradise Lost* describes Mammon as a fallen angel, a demon. Peter Binsfield, a Jesuit Priest in 1589, listed Mammon as one of the Seven Princes of Hell.

Jesus clearly states that Mammon is something people worship other than God. He says that it is impossible to have a spilt allegiance and yet many people don't believe Him. They worship Mammon in place of God and choose to do what Mammon leads them to do with their finances rather than what God leads them to do.

Look back at Proverbs 3 and see what God asks of us:

Proverbs 3:9-12 (NASB)
⁹ Honor the LORD from your wealth And from the first of all your produce; ¹⁰ So your barns will be filled with plenty And your vats will overflow with new wine. ¹¹ My son, do not reject the discipline of the LORD Or loathe His reproof, ¹² For whom the LORD loves He reproves, Even as a father corrects the son in whom he delights.

God is commanding us to worship Him by giving to Him financially. He asks us to give Him tithes and offerings. However, since we love our money so much, we try our best to find a way around this command and Mammon takes God's place in our lives.

I am intrigued that in the end times, the Anti-Christ will capture the hearts and minds of the people of the Earth through the control of money. Look at these two sections of Revelation.

Revelation 13:16-18 (NASB)
¹⁶ And he causes all, the small and the great, and the rich and the poor, and the free men and the slaves, to be given a mark on their right hand or on their forehead, ¹⁷ and he provides that no one will be able to buy or to sell, except the one who has the mark, either the name of the beast or the number of his name. ¹⁸ Here is wisdom. Let him who has understanding calculate the number of the beast, for the number is that of a man; and his number is six hundred and sixty-six.

Revelation 14:9-12 (NASB)
⁹ Then another angel, a third one, followed them, saying with a loud voice, "If anyone worships the beast and his image, and receives a mark on his forehead or on his hand, ¹⁰ he also will drink of the wine of the wrath of God, which is mixed in full strength in the cup of His anger; and he will be tormented with fire and brimstone in the presence of the holy angels and in the presence of the Lamb. ¹¹ And the smoke of their torment goes up forever and ever; they have no rest day and night, those who worship the beast and his image, and whoever receives the mark of his name." ¹² Here is the perseverance of the saints who keep the commandments of God and their faith in Jesus.

The word forehead is the Greek word, "meta opon" literally translated as "in the midst of the eye." John was told by Jesus that a day would come when people would not be able to buy or sell without having their hand or eye scanned. By taking this mark, they will be denying God and worshipping the Anti-Christ. Again, we see Satan using money to turn people away from God.

Some argue that God's command to give Him our tithes and offerings does not apply today because it was part of the Old Testament Law and Jesus came to abolish The Law. I have a couple of things to say about that. First, while I agree that we are no longer bound by the letter of The Law, we are to understand and live by the principles of it. Second, the principle of the tithe and first fruits predates the Law and is carried into the New Testament.

Abraham tithed prior to The Law being given (Genesis 14:18-20). In Hebrews 7:1-10 we are told that Abraham was tithing to Jesus and all of the Levitical priesthood did the same. The principle of the tithe is also found in the book of Proverbs. Proverbs is the wisdom of God for all time and all people. I find it ironic that everyone agrees that the commands and promises of Proverbs 3:5-8 apply to us and yet verses 9-12 are argued against. If Proverbs is the wisdom of God for all time and all people then the entire section applies to us. We must trust the Lord and not lean on our own understanding and we must honor Him from our wealth and give Him the first of our income.

Jesus commands us to tithe as well.

Matthew 23:23 (NLT)
[23] "What sorrow awaits you teachers of religious law and you Pharisees. Hypocrites! For you are careful to tithe even the tiniest income from your herb gardens, but you ignore the more important aspects of the law— justice, mercy, and faith. You should tithe, yes, but do not neglect the more important things."

Jesus tells the Pharisees that they are missing the most important aspects of living a life pleasing to God. They tithe but they do not practice love, justice, mercy, and grace. Jesus clearly tells them that they need to practice both the little things (tithing) and the big things.

Luke 16:10-13 (NASB)
[10] "He who is faithful in a very little thing is faithful also in much; and he who is unrighteous in a very little thing is unrighteous also in much. [11] Therefore if you have not been faithful in the use of unrighteous wealth, who will entrust the true riches to you? [12] And if you have not been faithful in the use of that which is another's, who will give you that which is your own? [13] No servant can serve two masters; for either he will hate the one and love the other, or else he will be devoted to one and despise the other. You cannot serve God and wealth."

There are four things that I want to point out from this passage of Scripture. First, if we are not faithful in the little things, we will not be faithful in the big things. Often I get asked, "How do I ensure that I will stay strong when the persecution of the last days come?" The answer is in this passage. If you are faithful now in your walk with Jesus, doing everything He has asked you to do, then you will be faithful when the hard times come.

Second, God has great things for us to experience but we have to show Him that we can be trusted with those things. Jesus says that if we are not faithful to Him with our finances, then we will not be entrusted with more important things from God. God will not give us "true riches," if we cannot be faithful in the area of finances. We are destined for a glorious purpose, but God is not going to entrust us with this purpose if we are not faithful in the little things.

Third, everything we have belongs to God. If we take on this perspective, it changes everything. Jesus, in verse 12, points out that everything we have belongs to God. When you became a Christian, you turned your life over to God, which means everything you own belongs to God. You also realize that everything you acquire comes from Him.

Deuteronomy 8:18 (NASB)
[18] "But you shall remember the LORD your God, for it is He who is giving you power to make wealth, that He may confirm His covenant which He swore to your fathers, as it is this day."

In light of this, when God asks for us to tithe to Him, we are actually returning the first ten percent of what already belongs to Him back to Him. This is why in Malachi 3:8-9, God says we are robbing Him when we do not give Him tithes and offerings.

Fourth, Jesus is telling us that the way we manage our finances reveals who or what we worship. When we are unfaithful in tithing, then we are serving Mammon rather than serving God.

In 1 Corinthians 9, Paul is making a case for why the Corinthian church should financially support him and those who teach the Word.

1 Corinthians 9:8-14 (NASB)
[8] I am not speaking these things according to human judgment, am I? Or does not the Law also say these things? [9] For it is written in the Law of Moses, "YOU SHALL NOT MUZZLE THE OX WHILE HE IS THRESHING." God is not concerned about oxen, is He? [10] Or is He speaking altogether

for our sake? Yes, for our sake it was written, because the plowman ought to plow in hope, and the thresher to thresh in hope of sharing the crops. ¹¹ If we sowed spiritual things in you, is it too much if we reap material things from you? ¹² If others share the right over you, do we not more? Nevertheless, we did not use this right, but we endure all things so that we will cause no hindrance to the gospel of Christ. ¹³ Do you not know that those who perform sacred services eat the food of the temple, and those who attend regularly to the altar have their share from the altar? ¹⁴ So also the Lord directed those who proclaim the gospel to get their living from the gospel.

In verse 13, Paul is referring to the tithe, which was given to the Levites so they could serve God in the Tabernacle and the Temple. He is saying that the Levites who did God's work in the Temple ate by means of the tithe. Paul carries this principle over into the Church saying that pastors should get paid by way of the tithe.

The tithe is instituted prior to The Law, is required by The Law, is commanded by Jesus, and is reiterated by Paul for the Church today. Even though I have made this case, I know that many will still try to find a theological argument that supports keeping God's money in our pockets. But, why would we want to rob God?

Malachi 3:8-9(NASB)
⁸ *"Will a man rob God? Yet you are robbing Me! But you say, 'How have we robbed You?' In tithes and offerings. ⁹ You are cursed with a curse, for you are robbing Me, the whole nation of you!"*

One of the saddest moments of my life is when I realized my son Tim was stealing from me. He was in Jr. High and was going through a rebellious phase. I caught him with money that I had left on the counter. My heart broke as the reality of the situation set in: my son whom I loved had stolen from me. It made no sense; I would have bought him anything he wanted and always made sure he had everything he needed. He had hurt me deeply.

God feels this same way when His children rob Him. He gave His one and only begotten Son for us and we yet we refuse to give Him a portion of what He blesses us with. He gives us everything we need and fulfills our heart's desires and yet we steal from Him. God asks us to test Him in this command. Stop robbing Him and unleash the blessings that He has for you. It really is a matter of the heart.

Matthew 6:19-21 (NASB)

[19] Do not store up for yourselves treasures on earth, where moth and rust destroy, and where thieves break in and steal. [20] But store up for yourselves treasures in heaven, where neither moth nor rust destroys, and where thieves do not break in or steal; [21] for where your treasure is, there your heart will be also.

If you want to discover what you love, look at where you spend your money. If God looked at your bank statements, would He know that you love Him or would He see that you love and worship Mammon? Jesus said that we cannot worship two entities at the same time. We must choose whom we will serve and that needs to be reflected in all areas of our lives. Look at these wonderful promises He makes to those who choose to be generous with Him.

Malachi 3:10-12 (NASB)

[10] "Bring the whole tithe into the storehouse, so that there may be food in My house, and test Me now in this," says the LORD of hosts, "if I will not open for you the windows of heaven and pour out for you a blessing until it overflows. [11] Then I will rebuke the devourer for you, so that it will not destroy the fruits of the ground; nor will your vine in the field cast its grapes," says the LORD of hosts. [12] "All the nations will call you blessed, for you shall be a delightful land," says the LORD of hosts.

Luke 6:38 (NASB)

[38] Give, and it will be given to you. They will pour into your lap a good measure—pressed down, shaken together, and running over. For by your standard of measure it will be measured to you in return.

2 Corinthians 9:6-15 (NASB)

[6] Now this I say, he who sows sparingly will also reap sparingly, and he who sows bountifully will also reap bountifully. [7] Each one must do just as he has purposed in his heart, not grudgingly or under compulsion, for God loves a cheerful giver. [8] And God is able to make all grace abound to you, so that always having all sufficiency in everything, you may have an abundance for every good deed; [9] as it is written, "HE SCATTERED ABROAD, HE GAVE TO THE POOR, HIS RIGHTEOUSNESS ENDURES FOREVER." [10] Now He who supplies seed to the sower and bread for food will supply and multiply your seed for sowing and increase the harvest of your righteousness; [11] you will be enriched in everything for all liberality, which through us is producing thanksgiving to God. [12] For the ministry of this service is not only fully supplying the needs of the saints, but is also overflowing through many thanksgivings to God. [13] Because of the proof given by this ministry, they will glorify God for your obedience

to your confession of the gospel of Christ and for the liberality of your contribution to them and to all, [14] while they also, by prayer on your behalf, yearn for you because of the surpassing grace of God in you. [15] Thanks be to God for His indescribable gift!

Chris is a member of Crossroads who takes his commitment to Christ seriously and as a result experienced God's promises. He and his wife Kim made the decision to trust God with their finances by tithing first when any income came in. God began a transformation in Chris' heart through his commitment to obedience in this area and gave him a new perspective. I want to share Chris's *Asah Shama* moment with you because it perfectly illustrates how obedience leads to the abundant life.

> I am in a sales environment with seven other sales people in my office. As sales people, our compensation is strictly commission based and at times, it can be very competitive and hostile. Throughout my two-and-a-half years of attending Crossroads, I have always attempted to apply the Bible-based messages you have shared to my life. My life has dramatically improved since I started attending (less debt, tithing, family, marriage). The things my heart wants have literally changed. However, as a salesman, jealousy was (and still is) a huge hurdle for me. My career is very competitive, and "what I should have got" or "could have got" was always eating at me. It was never enough. It was in direct contradiction to TRUSTING that God will take care of me. I was trying to take care of myself.

> On a Sunday a few months ago, one of your messages convicted me about this attitude and I prayed that I would learn to trust Jesus more. I prayed that if I were faithful in trusting him, he would take care of me.

> The following day, I received a passage from my mom via email which read, "It may not be YOUR need that I am seeking to fulfill; but of another through YOU." It was almost as if He knew this was going to be very hard for me, but he gave me this passage as a tool to keep my eyes on Him through this trial.

> Then the test started. NO SALES at all. Monday, Tuesday, nothing. Wednesday, nothing. Thursday, Friday, NOTHING. And it wasn't just nothing.

> It was in my face, obvious that something was off:

1. Getting a random phone call and missing walk-in business that would have been mine.

2. Checking a voice mail from an hour ago from a referral who wanted to come in and buy; calling back the customer; and having them answer their cell phone from my co-workers desk next to me who was already writing the business. They came in to the office but didn't ask for me.

3. When it was my co-worker's turn for walk-in business... GANGBUSTERS. When it was my turn... Ghost town. In seven years of working here, I had NEVER seen this. Not for SEVEN days straight!

This went on for a week. Every time I would get that knot in my stomach, I said that prayer, "It may not be YOUR need that I am seeking to fulfill; but of another through YOU." It was hard. However, every time I prayed that, I felt very peaceful. The knot left.

One week of TESTING. $0 in commission. I was worried because the bills were still coming.

Then came the miracle in a way only God can deliver.

A man came into my office and asked for me, not by name. He didn't know my name. He just described me, "I was told to ask for the Tall White Guy." We had never met before this.

When he came to my desk, his appearance was a bit intimidating. He had tattoos from his toes to his head. Very elaborate, yet intimidating. I introduced myself and he began to explain that he needed eight vehicles insured immediately. His insurance was canceling the next day and he needed it done right away.

Inside, I knew that this was equal to exactly one week of pay. All the sales that I had missed would be made up in this one sale.

Who was this guy? Tattoos everywhere! He even had a tattoo on his head that came down to his forehead that made it look like he had bangs.

I asked, "Do you have the registrations on any of the cars?" He had all eight registrations (no one ever has that with them when they come in)! I began to ask, "Jesus, is this you? Are you giving this to me for being faithful and fighting my jealous competitive urges and keeping my eyes on you?" As the man began to lay the registrations on my desk, the top of his head leaned toward me and I saw that the tattoo on his head wasn't bangs; it was the beard of Jesus! A full image of the face of Jesus was tattooed on the top of this man's shaved head, eyes open as if to answer my question!

This is truly an example of how God answers prayer. As you said on Sunday, your eyes have to be on Him -- striving to rid yourself of sin and follow Him. He knew my heart. He took care of me.

It wasn't until later that I realized that the wife of one of my co-workers was getting laid off from her teaching job and would need that extra money to make ends meet. Another co-worker was to be on medical leave and needed extra money. A third was going to have a baby and would need extra money in the next month. Truly, God fulfilled the need of another through me and fulfilled my needs as well.

Chapter Fourteen

Experience More

*"... 'I tell you the truth, when you did it to one of the least of these my brothers and sisters, you were doing it to me!' **Matthew 25:40 (NLT)***

"Do not be afraid. Leave your fears behind."

Life in the Old City was happening busily around me. I was aware of the bustling traffic and the noise from crowd of people talking all around me, but I could hear none of it. Stillness surrounded me and God's presence enveloped me. It was only me and God standing at the Western Wall when He audibly spoke these ever so powerful, personal words to me, His son.

One of the items on my bucket list ever since I had become a Christ follower was to go to Israel to walk Jesus' steps and see all the places I read about in Scripture. When the day finally came for me to fulfill this dream, I was ecstatic! Not only was I going to be able to see all of the sites talked about in the Bible, but I was going to get a chance to encourage Christians and help a church reaching Muslims in Ramallah.

Ramallah is a Palestinian city in the central West Bank. It is the capital of the Palestinian National Authority whose majority population is Islamic. It is a city filled with tension, separated from Israel by armed troops and high walls.

When we went through the checkpoint from Jerusalem into Ramallah and armed guards checked our vehicle, I could not help but pray. I felt like we had entered a war zone. Rubble from broken down buildings littered the streets and signs proclaiming allegiance to Allah were all around. And, there I was entering this hostile environment to preach to the last Evangelical Church left in this city. I was extremely uncomfortable and very aware of my need for Him. God had me right where He wanted me, completely dependent on Him and tuned into Him. I was ready to experience more.

He gave me more, more of Himself. He had taken me to a place outside of my comfort zone where I had to be completely reliant on Him, and in the midst of it He spoke a personal message to me. You see, I am one who struggles with worry and pessimism. I know the Bible tells us not to worry and to rejoice always, but I am human and I struggle. In that moment at the Western Wall, outside of my comfort zone, He met me and told me that it was time to embrace His promises, His presence and His truth.

While I will not tell you that everyone who chooses to experience more by going outside of their comfort zone will hear an audible voice, I promise that you will connect with God in a deeper way and will hear Him more clearly.

Proverbs 3:5-6 (NASB)
[5] Trust in the LORD with all your heart And do not lean on your own understanding. [6] In all your ways acknowledge Him, And He will make your paths straight.

Being outside of your comfort zone and fully committed to serving Him brings humility. When we are humble, we realize our need for God and are completely reliant on Him, trusting Him to guide us. When we live in these moments of uncertainty - serving the poor or sick in a foreign country; introducing Jesus to a group of people who hate Him; putting ourselves in harm's way to do what He as called us to do - we pray without ceasing. We are in constant connection with Him and we see Him and hear from Him.

Psalm 69:32 (NLT)
[32] The humble will see their God at work and be glad. Let all who seek God's help be encouraged.

In a recent round table discussion with a group of influential Christian leaders, we were discussing Spiritual formation. Each of us came from different Christian denominations and backgrounds, which meant we had opposing views on almost every subject. However, the one thing we all agreed on was this: The best way to connect with God is to go outside your comfort zone and serve Him.

Matthew 25:34-40 (NASB)
[34] Then the King will say to those on His right, 'Come, you who are blessed of My Father, inherit the kingdom prepared for you from the foundation of the world. [35] For I was hungry, and you gave Me something to eat; I was thirsty, and you gave Me something to drink; I was a stranger, and you invited Me in; [36] naked, and you clothed Me; I was sick, and you visited Me; I was in prison, and you came to Me.' [37] Then the

righteous will answer Him, 'Lord, when did we see You hungry, and feed You, or thirsty, and give You something to drink? [38] And when did we see You a stranger, and invite You in, or naked, and clothe You? [39] When did we see You sick, or in prison, and come to You?' [40] The King will answer and say to them, 'Truly I say to you, to the extent that you did it to one of these brothers of Mine, even the least of them, you did it to Me.'

Giving food to those who are hungry and water to those who are thirsty is giving food and water to Jesus. Visiting people who are sick and in prison is like visiting Jesus. Many of you are probably thinking that you don't want to go to the poorest of the poor, or to the sick, or to the prisoner. I want to challenge you to go anyway. This is what Jesus meant when He said, deny yourself, take up your cross, and follow Him. He has asked us to do these things, so we need to be obedient and do them.

My wife Pam is really good at "experiencing more." I remember during the time of the L.A. Riots, she challenged me to deny myself and step out of my comfort zone in a big way. We had walked out of our Wednesday night church service and the smell of fire filled the air. Someone yelled, "Los Angeles is on fire!" Pam and I ran home and turned on the news. We were shocked at violence and chaos that filled our TV screen. I kept thinking that this could not be real; it was too awful to be real. To my dismay, Pam looked over at me and said, "We need to go down there and help." I let her know that we would certainly NOT be going down there. She responded by telling me that she felt God calling our whole family to go and show His love to these people who needed it badly. This woman was determined! I was determined not to put my family in harm's way, but I thought I would do this in a very diplomatic way so as not to be the bad guy. Knowing it would be nearly impossible, I told her that if she could arrange a time when we were available and connect us with an organization, then we could go.

Pam prayed and contacted some L.A.P.D. officers we had connections with and, to my disappointment, she arranged for us to go to the very center of the riots to assist a church that was giving out food to the residents in the area who had no access to groceries. As we approached the riot area, the presence of spiritual darkness thickened. I was very aware of my powerlessness and my need for God. We drove through a National Guard barricade where I saw fully armed soldiers attempting to restore peace. Buildings had been reduced to smoldering ashes from the fires and the smell was nauseating. Devastation surrounded us.

When we stepped into the church, we were greeted like heroes. They were so encouraged that people cared enough to come and lend a hand.

These wonderful Christians loved us like long lost family. As we served the broken people of LA alongside our brothers and sisters in Christ, the presence of God was evident and powerful. His praise was on my lips and I was honored that He allowed me to serve Him in this way.

One day we will all stand before Him, will He say to you, "I was hungry and you gave me something to eat. I was thirsty and you gave me something to drink. I was in prison and you visited me. I was sick and you cared for me." Step out of your comfort zone and serve Him. Be obedient to His commands to care for the "least of these" and experience more!

You may be asking how you can experience more, and I'd like to make some suggestions to help you get started. Locally, you can help at a homeless shelter or in a neighborhood that is under resourced. Short-term mission trips are also great opportunities to minister throughout the world. Start with prayer and a heart that is willing to go wherever God sends you to experience more.

Chapter Fifteen

Love Like Jesus Loves

"A new commandment I give to you, that you love one another, even as I have loved you, that you also love one another. By this all men will know that you are My disciples, if you have love for one another."
John 13:34-35 (NASB)

Several years ago, Pam and I were on a short-term mission trip visiting a home in Africa for children with full-blown AIDS. When we walked into the playground area, the children rushed toward us wanting to play. Our entire team exuberantly accepted their invitation, running around the playground and loving on them. I stood on the perimeter talking with the leader of the home and noticed a little boy struggling to make his way over to the rest of the group. He walked slowly, and stopped every few steps to catch his breath. His weak state and the open sores on his head displayed the advanced stage of AIDS that wracked his body. Then, an angel came to his rescue; my wife, Pam, ran to him and swept him up into her arms. She held him close hugging him tight and kissed his sweet little face. The head caregiver looked at me and said, "That little boy is in heaven." My wife had never looked more beautiful to me than in that moment. She looked like Jesus, loving like He does.

God's greatest commandments are that we love Him and love others.

Matthew 22:37-40 (NASB)
[37] And He said to him, "'YOU SHALL LOVE THE LORD YOUR GOD WITH ALL YOUR HEART, AND WITH ALL YOUR SOUL, AND WITH ALL YOUR MIND.' [38] This is the great and foremost commandment. [39] The second is like it, 'YOU SHALL LOVE YOUR NEIGHBOR AS YOURSELF.' [40] On these two commandments depend the whole Law and the Prophets."

This is His greatest expectation of His children. He says that all of Scripture rests on the command to love. Paul reiterates this by saying that everything Christians teach and study should lead us to love.

1 Timothy 1:5 (NASB)

5 But the goal of our instruction is love from a pure heart and a good conscience and a sincere faith.

The true fruit of having a relationship with God is love. Notice that the goal of our instruction is not deeper knowledge, greater faith, or extreme sacrifice. The ultimate goal of our instruction is love. Life devoid of love is meaningless -- no greater than a loud irritating noise.

1 Corinthians 13:1-3 (NASB)

1 If I speak with the tongues of men and of angels, but do not have love, I have become a noisy gong or a clanging cymbal. 2 If I have the gift of prophecy, and know all mysteries and all knowledge; and if I have all faith, so as to remove mountains, but do not have love, I am nothing. 3 And if I give all my possessions to feed the poor, and if I surrender my body to be burned, but do not have love, it profits me nothing.

I have been around people who have a wealth of Bible knowledge and yet lack love and I sense the absence of Jesus. The proof of someone abiding in Christ is love. Love gives life meaning. God intentionally created us to live in a love relationship with Him and with others. We have a very high calling not only to love people the way we love ourselves but to love people the way that *He* loves people.

John 13:34-35 (NASB)

34 "A new commandment I give to you, that you love one another, even as I have loved you, that you also love one another. 35 By this all men will know that you are My disciples, if you have love for one another."

Jesus says that this extravagant love for one another will be our defining quality. People will know that we belong to Him because of the way we love each other. Remember, in John 8:31-32 Jesus said that we become His disciples by continuing in His Word. Now, we learn that all of the Word rests on loving God and loving others. Therefore, when we abide in Him we will love God and love people the way that Jesus loves them.

A college student from Crossroads walked into a grocery store just in time to see the fruit from a display tumble down to the floor. He saw a woman in traditional Islamic dress with three children trying to pick up the fruit and keep the rest from falling. She seemed a little overwhelmed as she attempted to keep track of her children and clean up the mess at the same time. This young college student instantly jumped to her rescue and then asked if she needed help with the rest of her shopping. With great appreciation in her eyes, she looked at him and asked, "Are you from that church in town that loves us?" He let her know that he was from Crossroads Church and she nodded in excitement and said, "Yes! That is the Church that loves us!"

The Islamic people in our area know Crossroads as the church that loves Muslims! It is our defining quality. When we love like Jesus loves, all will know that we are His disciples.

Jesus's standard of love is quite high. He loves extravagantly because love has the power to cover sins and bring unity. Love is the most important thing that we do.

1 Peter 4:8 (NASB)
8 Above all, keep fervent in your love for one another, because love covers a multitude of sins.

Colossians 3:14 (NASB)
14 Beyond all these things put on love, which is the perfect bond of unity...

Jesus loved God with His whole heart, mind and soul. One way that Jesus showed this type of love to His Father was by spending quality time with Him. He would stay up all night talking to His Father and would get up early in the morning to spend time with Him. He made it a point to get away from anything that would distract Him so that He could give His undivided attention to His Father.

Luke 5:16
16 But Jesus Himself would often slip away to the wilderness and pray.

Jesus also showed His love of God by doing everything that God commanded Him.

John 14:31 (NASB)
31 but so that the world may know that I love the Father, I do exactly as the Father commanded Me. Get up, let us go from here.

We love God the Father as Jesus loved Him when we do exactly as we are commanded. When the Father tells us to bring all of our tithes and offerings to Him, we obey. When we are told to love God with all of our heart, mind and soul, we love. When we are told to go into all the world and make disciples, we go. Obedience is motivated by love, and obedience is the evidence of love.

Jesus also gave us many examples of how to love people extravagantly as well. Let's look at some of the ways in which Jesus loved those with whom He came into contact:

- Jesus showed love by doing acts of kindness as He served them.
- Jesus showed His love by giving words of affirmation, encouraging and edifying people.
- Jesus showed His love by physically touching the blind, the leper, and other outcasts.
- Jesus showed His love by spending quality time with the disciples.
- Jesus showed His love by giving His life for us on the Cross.

If you've read *The Five Love Languages* by Dr. Gary Chapman, you probably noticed that Jesus showed love by way of each of the five Love Languages. According to Dr. Chapman, everyone has a preferred love language by which we feel loved. While we need all five expressions of love, one or two will be more meaningful than the others. Jesus loved people in each of these ways. He met peoples' needs and imparted value on them. In doing this, He filled them with love and motivated them to go and love others.

Jesus told His disciples that He came to serve and not to be served (Matthew 20:28). He showed them what this looks like by washing their feet and then told them to do the same for each other.

John 13:12-17 (NASB)
[12] So when He had washed their feet, and taken His garments and reclined at the table again, He said to them, "Do you know what I have done to you? [13] You call Me Teacher and Lord; and you are right, for so I am. [14] If I then, the Lord and the Teacher, washed your feet, you also ought to wash one another's feet. [15] For I gave you an example that you also should do as I did to you. [16] Truly, truly, I say to you, a slave is not greater than his master, nor is one who is sent greater than the one who sent him. [17] If you know these things, you are blessed if you do them."

Notice that we are only blessed if we do what He has told us to do -- the *Asah Shama*.

Jesus gave words of affirmation to Peter when He called Peter His rock. His edifying words were shared with all the disciples too. One of the most beautiful examples of this was the moment Jesus called the disciples his *friends*. He let them know that He loves them so much He is going to die for them.

John 15:12-15 (NASB)

[12] "This is My commandment, that you love one another, just as I have loved you. [13] Greater love has no one than this, that one lay down his life for his friends. [14] You are My friends if you do what I command you. [15] No longer do I call you slaves, for the slave does not know what his master is doing; but I have called you friends, for all things that I have heard from My Father I have made known to you."

There are eighteen recorded occasions in which Jesus used touch to show love to people. When the children came to Him, Jesus laid His hands on them and blessed them (Matthew 19:13-14). He also touched the lepers, the blind, and the dead because this was one of their greatest needs.

Jesus showed loved by spending quality time with the disciples. In Luke 22:15, He told them He earnestly desired to share the Passover meal with them. In Mark 6:31-32, after a time of intense ministry, He told them He wanted to take them to a secluded place. In Matthew 13, we see Jesus taking the time to explain His teachings to them. He spent three years spending quality time with His closest friends to prepare them, but also because He loved them.

Jesus ultimately showed love by giving His life as a gift for us that we might be forgiven of our sins and blessed with eternal life. There is no greater demonstration of love. God is the ultimate giver of gifts. He loves to bless His children by showing them His love in this way.

James 1:16-17 (NASB)

[16] Do not be deceived, my beloved brethren. [17] Every good thing given and every perfect gift is from above, coming down from the Father of lights, with whom there is no variation or shifting shadow.

Jesus loved people in the language that made them feel most valued. We need to love people in a way that makes them feel most loved. In high school, I unintentionally discovered that my wife Pam's love language was quality time. Being an immature young man, my conflict resolution skills were less than stellar. Pam had irritated me at school one day and instead of talking with her about it, I decided that I would make her pay during our date that evening by giving her the silent treatment. I picked her up and didn't say a word; instead I stared straight ahead and focused on the road. She was squirming inside, I was sure of it. We pulled up to a park and walked up to a grassy hill and sat down. The silence was so uncomfortable, but I would not be the first to talk.

After a while, I laid back and looked up at the stars. She followed suit. We stayed like that for what seemed like an eternity and I was a little perturbed at her ability to withstand the silence. All I wanted to do was talk (after all, I was destined to be a pastor), but I was not going to give in. She was suffering and would apologize to me soon enough. Finally, I couldn't take it anymore. I jumped up and said, "Well, it's getting late, I better get you home." Pam shocked me by jumping up, throwing her arms around my neck, and exclaiming, "Thank you so much for this! It was the best date we've ever had!" She went on and on about how I really knew her and how special I had made her feel by planning a date where we could spend quality time together. This was God's way of humbling me and teaching me how to best show love to my future wife!

Jesus loves people in a way that they best receive love, always looking to their best interest.

Philippians 2:3-11 (NASB)
3 Do nothing from selfishness or empty conceit, but with humility of mind regard one another as more important than yourselves; 4 do not merely look out for your own personal interests, but also for the interests of others. 5 Have this attitude in yourselves, which was also in Christ Jesus, 6 who, although He existed in the form of God, did not regard equality with God a thing to be grasped, 7 but emptied Himself, taking the form of a bond-servant, and being made in the likeness of men. 8 Being found in appearance as a man, He humbled Himself by becoming obedient to the point of death, even death on a cross. 9 For this reason also, God highly exalted Him, and bestowed on Him the name which is above every name, 10 so that at the name of Jesus EVERY KNEE WILL BOW, of those who are in heaven and on earth and under the earth, 11 and that every tongue will confess that Jesus Christ is Lord, to the glory of God the Father.

If we are going love like Jesus loves, then we will spend time with God and obey Him, and we will love people in a selfless manner. We will live lives of humility and love people in their language, regarding others' needs as more important than our own. This is very different from the way the world lives, but it is the best way to live. If you choose to love like this, you will experience the abundant life and understand the beauty of this command.

Great and Mighty Things for You

My friend was a good husband, a loving father, and a committed Christ follower, but something was missing. The frustration was written all over his face. He was doing all the right things, and there was no tragedy or hidden sin, but it just didn't seem to be enough. I will never forget the words he said to me over lunch one day, "I love God, but I thought being a Christian would be so much more."

Many Christians have these same sentiments. They love God and read the Bible, but don't see any parallel in their lives to what is happening in Scripture. This is not how God intends for our lives to be. Jesus tells us life with Him will be abundant (John 10:10). Paul says that life lived with Jesus is beyond imagination or description (2 Cor. 2:9). I have referred over and over to the promises of Jeremiah 33:3 where God promises to tell us great and mighty things. Look at what Paul says in Galatians 3:5,

Galatians 3:5 (NASB)
5 So then, does He who provides you with the Spirit and works miracles among you, do it by the works of the Law, or by hearing with faith?

Paul takes for granted that God is working miracles among them. He does not expect them to answer, "What miracles?" The argument he is making of a life lived in faith and not based on the law hinges on the great and mighty things they are experiencing. These miracles come by hearing with faith. Faith means trusting God and His Word. Trusting means we will take action on it (Asah) and then we will understand (Shama). The result is a miraculous life.

The purpose of this book is to point you to that miraculous life. As you live out a life of obedience to God's commands, you will be amazed at the promises He enacts in your life. This will happen in both big and small ways.

Zechariah 4:10a (NASB)

¹⁰ *"For who has despised the day of small things?"*

Do not overlook the little ways God works in our lives because we often will see Him take a little thing and make it big. We need to be faithful in both the little and the big things.

The Lord wants you to call to Him. He will answer. He will tell you great and mighty things you do not know. He is the one who will cause all things to work together for good if you love Him and live your life according to His purpose (Romans 8:28).

When I began to dig for the reasons my friend was not living the abundant life, the answers came. He was not consistent in intentionally meeting with God. He had never fasted in a way that would be honoring to the Lord. Rather than praying before he planned, he planned on his own without seeking God. Serving God by doing something outside of his comfort zone was not a priority. Although he was giving to God, he was not giving to God first. We talked through all of these things and he faced the truth of not being truly committed to God. I asked if he had a true hunger and thirst for righteousness and if he wanted to be who God wanted him to be. I am so thankful that my friend was open to correction and that he committed to living a life of complete obedience. He is amazed at the abundant life he is now experiencing. Each week, he has a new God story to share with me. He is seeing miracles happening and is being shown great and mighty things. There is no going back to the ordinary life.

God's promises are true! I know this because I experience them on a daily basis. Being in the hands of God and living the abundant life is all that God said it would be. I pray that you will choose the life of great and mighty things.

An Invitation

Earlier in this book, I mentioned that I never hold a church service without giving an invitation for people to come to know Jesus Christ. If you stumbled upon this book and you are not in a personal relationship with the Lord, He desires to have a relationship with you.

This is not about being religious; it is about having a relationship with God as Your Abba, your daddy. You were made to know God in this personal way and to live life with Him and for Him. He so loved you that He gave His only begotten Son (Jesus) for you. If you would believe in Him, then you will have eternal life (John 3:16). Eternal life is to truly know Him by experiencing Him (John 17:3).

When you commit your life to Him, you become a disciple of Jesus. A disciple is someone who learns from the one they follow and seeks to live life like Him. A disciple of Jesus acknowledges Him as their Lord because they love Him (Matthew 10:24-25).

If you want to enter into this personal relationship with the Lord, start by telling Him that you are ready to accept His invitation. Jesus says, He is standing at the door knocking and desires for you to say, "come in."

Revelation 3:20 (NASB)
[20] *Behold, I stand at the door and knock; if anyone hears My voice and opens the door, I will come in to him and will dine with him, and he with Me.*

I invite you to pray this prayer. Look at each line and say it with intentionality. Say it trusting He is with you now, hearing you, and ready to make you a new person.

Lord Jesus,
I know You died on the cross to forgive me and cleanse me of all my sins; to heal me of hurt and pain; and to free me from fear. I know you want me to be alive and to make me brand new. I want to be Yours.

So, I say yes! I want You and I want the life You have for me. Please come into my heart and fill me with Your love and with Your Spirit. I am Yours now. I pray these things in Jesus's name!

If you prayed that prayer, the next step is to make it known. You can do this by going on our web site (greatmightythings.com) and sharing your story. You also need to find a church that teaches the Bible as God's Word and let them know you have given your life to Christ.

Welcome to God's family! Get ready for the Great and Mighty Things God has for you!

Acknowledgements

I am grateful for all those who have been a part of the Crossroads story. Though it's not possible to name all of you, I know God cares about the effort you have given to make Crossroads the church it is today.

Thank you to Taleah Murray, who spent countless hours editing this book with the desire for it to read what I was hoping to say. This book would not be a reality without your commitment to the Lord and belief that His Word and ways are always right. You are an example of service with unwavering faith.

Thank you to Mike Long who felt and obeyed the call of God to partner with me in ministry at CCV and again at Crossroads when the situation was dire. Your wisdom and cherished friendship in those first few months before you joined us on staff will not be forgotten. I am thankful for your passion and optimism that kept us all believing God would get us through.

Thank you to Blake Ryan for diving into a mess I was not sure could be cleaned up. You served with an integrity and passion that could only come from your love for the Lord and His Church. I am confident God will reward your blood, sweat and tears.

Thank you to Peter McGowan and PlainJoe Studios. Peter, you have always served the Lord and others with a contagious passion. I am in awe of your selflessness and dedication to provide Crossroads with an excellence we could not afford at one time. I will forever value our friendship.

Thank you to Todd Horne for editing this book and doing so with a love and devotion to the Lord and Crossroads. Your friendship in the early days of my leading here was a sign to me of our bright future as a church. Having you involved in the editing of this story brought me great joy and comfort in moving forward.

Thank you to the Crossroads family, who in the early days of my coming rallied because they loved the Lord and wanted to see God's great plan for this church move forward. I praise God that I get to be with you as we seek to bring all people to a passionate commitment to Christ, His Cause and His Community.

Thank you to my wife, Pam Booher, for being the most Christ-like and faith-filled person I know. I do not deserve you, but I love and treasure you as a gift from God. You inspire and encourage me to believe God always "can."

Most of all, I want to thank my Lord and Savior Jesus Christ who forgave me, cleansed me and changed me. I love Him and am amazed that He has called me to serve Him.

24:7 Bible Reading Plan

Your personal reading schedule to take you through the entire Bible within one year—the Old Testament once and the New Testament twice.

OCTOBER
1. Proverbs 1; Psalm 1-2
2. Proverbs 2; Psalm 3-4
3. Proverbs 3; Psalm 5-6
4. Proverbs 4; Psalm 7-8
5. Proverbs 5; Psalm 9
6. Proverbs 6; Psalm 10
7. Proverbs 7; Psalm 11-13
8. Proverbs 8; Psalm 14-16
9. Proverbs 9; Psalm 17
10. Proverbs 10; Psalm 18
11. Proverbs 11; Psalm 19-20
12. Proverbs 12; Psalm 21-22
13. Proverbs 13; Psalm 23-24
14. Proverbs 14; Psalm 25-26
15. Proverbs 15; Psalm 27-28
16. Proverbs 16; Psalm 29-30
17. Proverbs 17; Psalm 31
18. Proverbs 18; Psalm 32-33
19. Proverbs 19; Psalm 34-35
20. Proverbs 20; Psalm 36
21. Proverbs 21; Psalm 37
22. Proverbs 22; Psalm 38
23. Proverbs 23; Psalm 39
24. Proverbs 24; Psalm 40
25. Proverbs 25; Psalm 41
26. Proverbs 26; Psalm 42
27. Proverbs 27; Psalm 43
28. Proverbs 28; Psalm 44
29. Proverbs 29; Psalm 45-46
30. Proverbs 30; Psalm 47-48
31. Proverbs 31; Psalm 49-50

NOVEMBER
1. Proverbs 1; Psalm 51
2. Proverbs 2; Psalm 52-53
3. Proverbs 3; Psalm 54-55
4. Proverbs 4; Psalm 56-57
5. Proverbs 5; Psalm 58-59
6. Proverbs 6; Psalm 60-61
7. Proverbs 7; Psalm 62-63
8. Proverbs 8; Psalm 64-65
9. Proverbs 9; Psalm 66-67
10. Proverbs 10; Psalm 68
11. Proverbs 11; Psalm 69
12. Proverbs 12; Psalm 70-71
13. Proverbs 13; Psalm 72
14. Proverbs 14; Psalm 73
15. Proverbs 15; Psalm 74
16. Proverbs 16; Psalm 75-76
17. Proverbs 17; Psalm 77
18. Proverbs 18; Psalm 78
19. Proverbs 19; Psalm 79-80
20. Proverbs 20; Psalm 81-82
21. Proverbs 21; Psalm 83-84
22. Proverbs 22; Psalm 85-86
23. Proverbs 23; Psalm 87-88
24. Proverbs 24; Psalm 89
25. Proverbs 25; Psalm 90-91
26. Proverbs 26; Psalm 92-94
27. Proverbs 27; Psalm 95-96
28. Proverbs 28; Psalm 97-98
29. Proverbs 29; Psalm 99
30. Proverbs 30-31; Psalm 100

DECEMBER
1. Proverbs 1; Psalm 101-102
2. Proverbs 2; Psalm 103
3. Proverbs 3; Psalm 104
4. Proverbs 4; Psalm 105
5. Proverbs 5; Psalm 106
6. Proverbs 6; Psalm 107
7. Proverbs 7; Psalm 108-109
8. Proverbs 8; Psalm 110-111

9. Proverbs 9; Psalm 112-113
10. Proverbs 10; Psalm 114-115
11. Proverbs 11; Psalm 116-117
12. Proverbs 12; Psalm 118
13. Proverbs 13; Psalm 119
14. Proverbs 14; Psalm 120-121
15. Proverbs 15; Psalm 122-123
16. Proverbs 16; Psalm 124-125
17. Proverbs 17; Psalm 126-127
18. Proverbs 18; Psalm 128-129
19. Proverbs 19; Psalm 130-131
20. Proverbs 20; Psalm 132-133
21. Proverbs 21; Psalm 134-135
22. Proverbs 22; Psalm 136-137
23. Proverbs 23; Psalm 138-139
24. Proverbs 24; Psalm 140-141
25. Proverbs 25; Psalm 142-143
26. Proverbs 26; Psalm 144-145
27. Proverbs 27; Psalm 146
28. Proverbs 28; Psalm 147
29. Proverbs 29; Psalm 148
30. Proverbs 30; Psalm 149
31. Proverbs 31; Psalm 150

JANUARY
1. Gen. 1,2; Luke 1
2. Gen. 3-5; Luke 2
3. Gen. 6-8; Luke 3
4. Gen. 9-11; Luke 4
5. Gen. 12-14; Luke 5
6. Gen. 15-17; Luke 6
7. Gen. 18, 19; Ps. 3; Luke 7
8. Gen. 20-22; Luke 8
9. Gen. 23, 24; Luke 9
10. Gen. 25, 26; Ps. 6; Luke 10
11. Gen. 27, 28; Ps. 4; Luke 11
12. Gen. 29, 30; Luke 12
13. Gen. 31-33; Luke 13
14. Gen. 34-36; Luke 14
15. Gen. 37, 38; Ps. 7; Luke 15
16. Gen. 39-41; Luke 16
17. Gen. 39-41; Ps. 5; Luke 17
18. Gen. 39-41; Luke 18
19. Gen. 39-41; Ps. 10; Luke 19
20. Gen. 39-41; Ps. 8; Luke 20
21. Ex. 1, 2; Ps. 88; Luke 21
22. Ex. 3-5; Luke 22
23. Ex. 6-8; Luke 23
24. Ex. 9-11; Luke 24

25. Ex. 12, 13; Ps. 21; Acts 1
26. Ex. 14-16; Acts 2
27. Ex. 17-20; Acts 3
28. Ex. 21, 22; Ps. 12; Acts 4
29. Ex. 23, 24; Ps. 14; Acts 5
30. Ex. 25-27; Acts 6
31. Ex. 28-29; Acts 7

FEBRUARY
1. Ex. 30-32; Acts 8
2. Ex. 33, 34; Ps. 16; Acts 9
3. Ex. 35, 36; Acts 10
4. Ex. 37, 38; Ps. 19; Acts 11
5. Ex. 39, 40; Ps. 15; Acts 12
6. Lev. 1-3; Acts 13
7. Lev. 4-6; Acts 14
8. Lev. 7-9; Acts 15
9. Lev. 10-12; Acts 16
10. Lev. 13, 14; Acts 17
11. Lev. 15-17; Acts 18
12. Lev. 18, 19; Ps. 13; Acts 19
13. Lev. 20-22; Acts 20
14. Lev. 23, 24; Ps. 24; Acts 21
15. Lev. 25; Ps. 25-26; Acts 22
16. Lev. 26, 27; Acts 23
17. Num. 1, 2; Acts 24
18. Num. 3, 4; Acts 25
19. Num. 5, 6; Ps. 22; Acts 26
20. Num. 7; Ps. 23; Acts 27
21. Num. 8, 9; Acts 28
22. Num. 10, 11; Ps. 27; Mark 1
23. Num. 12, 13; Ps. 90; Mark 2
24. Num. 14-16; Mark 3
25. Num. 17, 18; Ps. 29; Mark 4
26. Num. 19, 20; Ps. 28; Mark 5
27. Num. 21-23; Mark 6, 7
28. Num. 24-27; 1 Cor. 13 22
29. Exodus 24; Acts 2

MARCH
1. Num. 28-29; Mark 8
2. Num. 30-31; Mark 9
3. Num. 32, 33; Mark 10
4. Num. 34-36; Mark 11
5. Duet. 1, 2; Mark 12
6. Duet. 3, 4; Ps. 36; Mark 13
7. Duet. 5, 6; Ps. 43; Mark 14
8. Duet. 7-9; Mark 15
9. Duet. 10-12; Mark 16

10. Duet. 13-15; Gal. 1
11. Duet. 16-18; Ps. 38; Gal. 2
12. Duet. 19-21; Gal. 3
13. Duet. 22-24; Gal. 4
14. Duet. 25-27; Gal. 5
15. Duet. 28, 29; Gal. 6
16. Duet. 30, 31; Ps. 40; 1 Cor. 1
17. Duet. 32-34; 1 Cor. 2
18. Josh. 1, 2; Ps. 37; 1 Cor. 3
19. Josh. 3-6; 1 Cor. 4
20. Josh. 7, 8; Ps. 69; 1 Cor. 5
21. Josh. 9-11; 1 Cor. 6
22. Josh. 12-14; 1 Cor. 7
23. Josh. 15-17; 1 Cor. 8
24. Josh. 18-20; 1 Cor. 9
25. Josh. 21, 22; Ps. 47; 1 Cor. 10
26. Josh. 23, 24; Ps. 44; 1 Cor. 11
27. Judg. 1-3; 1 Cor. 12
28. Judg. 4, 5; Ps. 39, 40; 1 Cor. 13
29. Judg. 6, 7; Ps. 52; 1 Cor. 14
30. Judg. 8; Ps. 42; 1 Cor. 15
31. Judg. 9, 10; Ps. 49; 1 Cor. 16

APRIL

1. Judg. 11,12; Ps. 50; 2 Cor. 1
2. Judg. 13-16; 2 Cor. 2
3. Judg. 17, 18; Ps. 89; 2 Cor. 3
4. Judg. 19-21; 2 Cor. 4
5. Ruth. 1, 2; Ps. 53, 61; 2 Cor. 5
6. Ruth. 3, 4; Ps. 64, 65; 2 Cor. 6
7. 1 Sam. 1, 2; Ps. 66; 2 Cor. 7
8. 1 Sam. 3-5; Ps. 77; 2 Cor. 8
9. 1 Sam. 6, 7; Ps. 72; 2 Cor. 9
10. 1 Sam. 8-10; 2 Cor. 10
11. 1 Sam. 11, 12; 1 Chr. 1; 2 Cor. 11
12. 1 Sam. 13; 1 Chr. 2, 3; 2 Cor. 12
13. 1 Sam. 14; 1 Chr. 4; 2 Cor. 13
14. 1 Sam. 15, 16; 1 Chr. 5; Mt. 1
15. 1 Sam. 17; Ps. 9; Mt. 2
16. 1 Sam. 18; 1 Chr. 6; Ps. 11; Mt. 3
17. 1 Sam. 19; 1 Chr. 7; Ps. 59; Mt. 4
18. 1 Sam. 20; Ps. 34; Mt. 5
19. 1 Sam. 22; Ps. 17, 35; Mt. 6
20. 1 Sam. 23; Ps. 31, 54; Mt. 7
21. 1 Sam. 24; Ps. 57,58; 1 Chr. 8; Mt. 8
22. 1 Sam. 25, 26; Ps. 63; Mt. 9
23. 1 Sam. 27; Ps. 141; 1 Chr. 9; Mt. 10
24. 1 Sam. 28, 29; Ps. 109; Mt. 11
25. 1 Sam. 30, 31; 1 Chr. 10; Mt. 12

26. 2 Sam. 1; Ps. 140; Mt. 13
27. 2 Sam. 2; 1 Chr. 11; Ps. 142; Mt. 14
28. 2 Sam. 3; 1 Chr. 12; Mt. 15
29. 2 Sam. 4, 5; Ps. 139; Mt. 16
30. 2 Sam. 6; 1 Chr. 13; Ps. 68; Mt. 17

MAY

1. 1 Chr. 14, 15; Ps. 132; Mt. 18
2. 1 Chr. 14, 16; Ps. 106; Mt. 19
3. 2 Sam. 7; 1 Chr. 17; Ps. 2; Mt. 20
4. 2 Sam. 8, 9; 1 Chr. 18, 19; Mt. 21
5. 2 Sam. 10; 1 Chr. 20; Ps. 20; Mt. 22
6. 2 Sam. 11, 12; Ps. 51; Mt. 23
7. 2 Sam. 13, 14; Mt. 24
8. 2 Sam. 15, 16; Ps. 32; Mt. 25
9. 2 Sam. 17; Ps. 71; Mt. 26
10. 2 Sam. 18; Ps. 56; Mt. 27
11. 2 Sam. 19, 20; Ps. 55; Mt. 28
12. 2 Sam. 21-23; 1 Th. 1
13. 2 Sam. 24; 1 Chr. 21; Ps. 30; 1 Th. 2
14. 1 Chr. 22-24; 1 Th. 3
15. 1 Chr. 25-27; 1 Th. 4
16. 1 Ki. 1; 1 Chr. 28; Ps. 91; 1 Th. 5
17. 1 Ki. 2; 1 Chr. 29; Ps. 95; 2 Th. 1
18. 1 Ki. 3; 2 Chr. 1; Ps. 78; 2 Th. 2
19. 1 Ki. 4, 5; 2 Chr. 2; Ps. 101; 2 Th. 3
20. 1 Ki. 6; 2 Chr. 3; Ps. 97; Rom. 1
21. 1 Ki. 7; 2 Chr. 4; Ps. 98; Rom. 2
22. 1 Ki. 8; 2 Chr. 5; Ps. 99; Rom. 3
23. 2 Chr. 6, 7; Ps. 135; Rom. 4
24. 1 Ki. 9; 2 Chr. 8; Ps. 136; Rom. 5
25. 1 Ki. 10, 11; 2 Chr. 9; Rom. 6
26. Prov. 1-3; Rom. 7
27. Prov. 4-6; Rom. 8
28. Prov. 7-9; Rom. 9
29. Prov. 10-12; Rom. 10
30. Prov. 13-15; Rom. 11
31. Prov. 16-18; Rom. 12

JUNE

1. Prov. 19-21; Rom. 13
2. Prov. 22-24; Rom. 14
3. Prov. 25-27; Rom. 15
4. Prov. 28, 29; Ps. 60; Rom. 16
5. Prov. 30-31; Ps. 33; Eph. 1
6. Ecc. 1-3; Ps. 45; Eph. 2
7. Ecc. 4-6; Ps. 18; Eph. 3
8. Ecc. 7-9; Eph. 4
9. Ecc. 10-12; Ps. 94; Eph. 5

10. Song 1-4; Eph. 6
11. Song 5-8; Phil.1
12. 1 Ki. 12; 2 Chr. 10, 11; Phil. 2
13. 1 Ki. 13, 14; 2 Chr. 12; Phil. 3
14. 1 Ki. 15; 2 Chr. 13, 14; Phil. 4
15. 1 Ki. 16; 2 Chr. 15, 16; Col. 1
16. 1 Ki. 17-19; Col. 2
17. 1 Ki. 20, 21; 2 Chr. 17; Col. 3
18. 1 Ki. 21; 2 Chr. 18, 19; Col. 4
19. 2 Ki. 1-3; Ps. 82; 1 Tim. 1
20. 2 Ki. 4, 5; Ps. 83; 1 Tim. 2
21. 2 Ki. 6, 7; 2 Chr. 20; 1 Tim. 3
22. 2 Ki. 8, 9; 2 Chr. 21; 1 Tim. 4
23. 2 Ki. 10; 2 Chr. 22, 23; 1 Tim. 5
24. 2 Ki. 11, 12; 2 Chr. 24; 1 Tim. 6
25. Joel 1-3; 2 Tim. 1
26. Jon. 1-4; 2 Tim. 2
27. 2 Ki. 13, 14; 2 Chr. 25; 2 Tim. 3
28. Amos 1-3; Ps. 80; 2 Tim. 4
29. Amos 4-6; Ps. 86; Tit. 1
30. Amos 7-9; Ps. 104; Tit. 2

JULY

1. Is. 1-3; Tit. 3
2. Is. 4, 5; Ps. 115, 116; Jude
3. Is. 6, 7; Chr. 26, 27; Philem.
4. 2 Ki. 15, 16; Hos. 1; Heb.1
5. Hos. 2-5; Heb. 2
6. Hos. 6-9; Heb. 3
7. Hos. 10-12; Ps. 73; Heb. 4
8. Hos. 13, 14; Ps. 100, 102; Heb. 5
9. Mic. 1-4; Heb. 6
10. Mic. 5-7; Heb. 7
11. Is. 8-10; Heb. 8
12. Is. 11-14; Heb. 9
13. Is. 15-18; Heb. 10
14. Is. 19-21; Heb. 11
15. Is. 22-24; Heb. 12
16. Is. 25-28; Heb. 13
17. Is. 29-31; Jas. 1
18. Is. 32-35; Jas. 2
19. 2 Ki. 17; 2 Chr. 28; Ps. 46; Ias. 3
20. 2 Chr. 29-31; Jas. 4
21. 2 Ki. 18, 19; 2 Chr. 32; Jas. 5
22. Is. 36, 37; Ps. 76; 1 Pet. 1
23. 2 Ki. 20; Is. 38, 39; Ps. 75; 1 Pet. 2
24. Is. 40-42; 1 Pet. 3
25. Is. 43-45; 1 Pet. 4
26. Is. 46-49; 1 Pet. 5

27. Is. 50-52; Ps. 92; 2 Pet. 1
28. Is. 53-56; 2 Pet. 2
29. Is. 57-59; Ps. 103; 2 Pet. 3
30. Is. 60-62; Jn. 1
31. Is. 63, 64; Ps. 107; John 2

AUGUST

1. Is. 65, 66; Ps. 62; Jn. 3
2. 2 Ki. 21; 2 Chr. 33; Jn. 4
3. Nah. 1-3; John 5
4. 2 Ki. 22; 2 Chr. 34; Jn. 6
5. 2 Ki. 23; 2 Chr. 35; Jn. 7
6. Hab. 1-3; Jn. 8
7. Zeph. 1-3; Jn. 9
8. Jer. 1, 2; Jn. 10
9. Jer. 3, 4; Jn. 11
10. Jer. 5, 6; Jn. 12
11. Jer. 7-9; Jn. 13
12. Jer. 10-12; Jn. 14
13. Jer. 13-15; Jn. 15
14. Jer. 16, 17; Ps. 96; Jn. 16
15. Jer. 18-20; Ps. 93; Jn. 17
16. 2 Ki. 24; Jer. 22; Ps. 112; Jn.18
17. Jer. 23, 25; Jn. 19
18. Jer. 26, 35, 36; Jn. 20
19. Jer. 45-47; Ps. 105; Jn. 21
20. Jer. 48, 49; Ps. 67; 1 Jn. 1
21. Jer. 21, 24, 27; Ps. 118; 1 Jn. 2
22. Jer. 28-30; 1 Jn. 3
23. Jer. 31, 32; 1 Jn. 4
24. Jer. 33, 34; Ps. 74; 1 Jn. 5
25. Jer. 37-39; Ps. 79; 2 Jn.
26. Jer. 50, 51; 3 Jn.
27. Jer. 52; Rev. 1; Ps. 143, 144
28. Ezek. 1-3; Rev. 2
29. Ezek. 4-7; Rev. 3
30. Ezek. 8-11; Rev. 4
31. Ezek. 12-14; Rev. 5

SEPTEMBER

1. Ezek. 15, 16; Ps. 70; Rev. 6
2. Ezek. 17-19; Rev. 7
3. Ezek. 20, 21; Ps. 111; Rev. 8
4. Ezek. 22-24; Rev. 9
5. Ezek. 25-28; Rev. 10
6. Ezek. 29-32; Rev. 11
7. 2 Ki. 25; 2 Chr. 36; Jer. 40, 41; Rev. 12
8. Jer. 42-44; Ps. 48; Rev. 13
9. Lam. 1, 2; Obad. Rev. 14

10. Lam. 3-5; Rev. 15
11. Dan. 1, 2; Rev. 16
12. Dan. 3, 4; Ps. 81; Rev. 17
13. Ezek. 33-35; Rev. 18
14. Ezek. 36, 37; Ps. 110; Rev. 19
15. Ezek. 38, 39; Ps. 145; Rev. 20
16. Ezek. 40, 41; Ps. 128; Rev. 21
17. Ezek. 42-44; Rev. 22
18. Ezek. 45, 46; Lk. 1
19. Ezek. 47, 48; Lk. 2
20. Dan. 5, 6; Ps. 130; Lk. 3
21. Dan. 7, 8; Ps. 137; Lk.4
22. Dan. 9, 10; Ps. 123; Lk.5
23. Dan. 11, 12; Lk. 6
24. Ezra 1; Ps. 84, 85; Lk.7
25. Ezra 2, 3; Lk. 8
26. Ezra 4; Ps. 113, 127; Lk. 9
27. Hag. 1, 2; Ps. 129; Lk. 10
28. Zech. 1-3; Lk. 11
29. Zech. 4-6; Lk. 12
30. Zech. 7-9; Lk. 13

OCTOBER
1. Zech. 10-12; Ps. 126; Lk. 14
2. Zech. 13, 14; Ps. 147; Lk. 15
3. Ezra 5, 6; Ps. 138; Lk.16
4. Est. 1, 2; Ps. 150; Lk. 17
5. Est. 3-8; Lk. 18
6. Est. 9-10; Lk. 19
7. Ezra 7, 8; Lk. 20
8. Ezra 9, 10; Ps. 131; Lk. 21
9. Neh. 1, 2; Ps. 133, 134; Lk. 22
10. Neh. 3, 4; Lk. 23
11. Neh. 5, 6; Ps. 146; Lk. 24
12. Neh. 7, 8; Acts 1
13. Neh. 9, 10; Acts 2
14. Neh. 11, 12; Ps, 1; Acts 3
15. Neh. 13; Mal. 1, 2; Acts 4
16. Mal. 3, 4; Ps. 148; Acts 5
17. Job 1, 2; Acts 6, 7
18. Job 3, 4; Acts 8, 9
19. Job 5; Ps. 108; Acts 10, 11
20. Job 6-8; Acts 12
21. Job 9, 10; Acts 13, 14
22. Job 11, 12; Acts 15, 16
23. Job 13, 14; Acts 17, 18
24. Job 15; Acts 19, 20
25. Job 16; Acts 21-23
26. Job 17; Acts 24-26

27. Job 18; Ps. 114; Acts 27, 28
28. Job 19; Mark 1, 2
29. Job 20; Mark 3, 4
30. Job 21; Mark 5, 6
31. Job 22; Mark 7, 8

NOVEMBER
1. Ps. 21; Mark 9, 10
2. Job 23, 24; Mark 11, 12
3. Job 25; Mark 13, 14
4. Job 26, 27; Mark 15, 16
5. Job 28, 29; Gal. 1, 2
6. Job 30; Ps. 120; Gal. 3, 4
7. Job 31, 32; Gal. 5, 6
8. Job 33; 1 Cor. 1-3
9. Job 34; 1 Cor. 4-6
10. Job 35, 36; 1 Cor. 7, 8
11. Ps, 122; 1 Cor. 9-11
12. Job 37, 18; Cor. 12
13. Job 39, 40; 1Cor. 13, 14
14. Ps. 149; 1 Cor. 15, 16
15. Job 41, 42; 2 Cor. 1, 2
16. 2 Cor. 3-6
17. 2 Cor. 7-10
18. Ps. 124; 2 Cor. 11-13
19. Mt. 1-4
20. Mt. 5-7
21. Mt. 8-10
22. Mt. 11-13
23. Mt. 14-16
24. Mt. 17-19
25. Mt. 20-22
26. Mt. 23-25
27. Ps. 125; Mt. 26, 27
28. Mt. 28; 1 Th. 1-3
29. 1 Th. 4, 5; 2 Th. 1-3
30. Romans 1-4

DECEMBER
1. Rom. 5-8
2. Rom. 9-12
3. Rom. 13-16
4. Eph. 1-4
5. Eph. 5, 6; Ps. 119:1-80
6. Phil. 1-4
7. Col. 1-4
8. 1 Tim. 1-4
9. 1 Tim. 5, 6; Tit. 1-3
10. 2 Tim. 1-4

11. Philem; Heb. 1-4
12. Heb. 5-8
13. Heb. 9-11
14. Heb. 12, 13; Jude
15. Jas. 1-5
16. 1 Pet. 1-5
17. 2 Pet. 1-3; Jn. 1
18. Jn. 2-4
19. Jn. 5, 6
20. Jn. 7, 8
21. Jn. 9-11
22. Jn. 12-14
23. Jn. 15-18
24. Jn. 19-21
25. 1 Jn. 1-5
26. Ps. 117, 119:81-176; 2 Jn; 3 Jn.
27. Rev. 1-4
28. Rev. 5-9
29. Rev. 10-14
30. Rev. 15-18
31. Rev. 19-2